CW00407417

THE
Sᴛ HELENS
SAINTS
MISCELLANY

Dᴀʀʀᴇɴ Pʜɪʟʟɪᴘs

First published 2010

The History Press
The Mill, Brimscombe Port
Stroud, Gloucestershire, GL5 2QG
www.thehistorypress.co.uk

British Library Cataloguing in Publication Data.
A catalogue record for this book is available from the British Library.

ISBN 978 0 7524 5746 8

Typesetting and origination by The History Press
Printed in Great Britain

REBELS FOR THE CAUSE

St Helens were one of the 21 clubs which decided to form the Northern Rugby Football Union on 29 August 1895 when a motion to leave the Rugby Football Union was carried at Huddersfield's George Hotel. The over-eager application of amateur status and, particularly, the prohibition of making up the wages of those who had to take time away from their work with 'broken time payments' was a huge issue – though not the sole grievance – to the northern clubs who drew their playing resources from ordinary working men. They thought it fair to pay six shillings compensation in order not to cause hardship and refused to accept this conferred professionalism on their players. Especially as the RFU had allowed others payment. That row had bubbled for almost two years. Fewer problems were encountered in the south where the medical, legal and other well remunerated occupations dominated the playing pool.

However, there was also perhaps an ulterior motive. Clubs from Lancashire and Yorkshire particularly were dominating the sport so measures were put in place to restrict their perceived advantages – and then enforced vigorously. It is notable that shorn of their Lancastrian and Yorkshire contingent, England's Union team didn't win the International Championship, now known as the Six Nations, until 1910.

Without doubt inducements were on offer, and to make such disbursements, entrance fees were prime among the measures used to raise funds. But after years of having one arm forced behind their back, the north rebelled. Yorkshire clubs were first to murmur about a split and then Lancashire's top sides gathered in Manchester and pledged their support. Within 48 hours the game was split across two factions. Only Dewsbury decided to stay, although after three years of withering on the RFU's vine and winding up their rugby team, they claimed a place within the Northern Union. Draconian action by Union's governing body had seen bans hit many purely recreational clubs whose only crime was to maintain relations with defectors, even those who remained amateur but did make broken time payments. An inevitable consequence was to increase the Northern Union's membership.

LICENSED HEADQUARTERS

Like many Northern Union teams, St Helens listed their headquarters as a public house, the club's hostelry of choice being the Duke of Cambridge, appropriately and by no small coincidence situated on Duke Street. There were very few exceptions to this general rule. The club used the Talbot Hotel for many years after. It would also serve as a changing room ahead of games.

ROYALS AND HORNETS

Regardless of the code, a fairly unrecognisable form of rugby by modern standards formed St Helens' baptism under RFU patronage towards the end of January 1874. A team consisting of 20 players took on Liverpool Royal Infirmary who were a number of players short but still had the better of exchanges registering five tries to nil. However, as the try earned no points at the time, merely the right for a side to try a kick at goal, the final score was level, the

Royals failing to land any of their attempts. The game at the Recreation Cricket Ground at Boundary Road took place a couple of months after St Helens were founded by William Douglas Herman, a chemist at Pilkington's Crown Glassworks. Mr Herman became chairman by acclaim at a public meeting held at the Fleece Hotel on 19 November 1873 and should have played in that first game as captain. He was forced to miss out due to his move to the town taking place on the same day.

As a Northern Union club, Saints opened up a new era and ultimately the course of a whole new game, entertaining Rochdale Hornets. Winger Bob Doherty who had left Union side Kendal Hornets to gain pay for his talents scored the club's first ever Rugby League try in the 8–3 win. Intercepting in the final quarter of the field he sprinted through and though the finish was a bit of a tumble, the quality of his play was superb. Lock Peter Dale was the only other home player to cross the line. Billy Cross, another former Kendal man, completed the scoring with a goal. Eventually those pioneering players drifted away from the club or went into retirement. The last to call it a day was Billy Briers in 1912 at the ripe old age of 37. Alternating between backs and forward line, he clocked up 515 appearances.

IN THE DOCK

Those hard-won points against the Hornets were later forfeited due to one player, Bill Jacques, not having been properly registered ahead of the game. The half-back was still effectively a Hull man. Because of this the club became the first to receive the disciplinary sanction of a points deduction.

HOME SWEET HOME

Until the end of the 2010 season St Helens will have played at their Knowsley Road home for 120 years. They moved from City Road in 1890 and defeated Manchester Rangers in the first match played at the venue on 6 September of that year.

SUPPORTERS LEND A HAND

Many of the first ground improvements at Knowsley Road came with substantial assistance from the supporters' club formed by Jesse Sneekes. They wanted to build a covered stand down the Popular side. This wooden structure was replaced by a steel and iron construction in 1962 with the old edifice transported down the road to Liverpool City's Knotty Ash ground. The pavilion, located at the Dunriding Lane end, received a ceremonial opening by the Rugby Football League's Honorary President, Lord Derby, on Boxing Day 1920. Ribbon-cutting took place prior to a meeting with Wigan and the building remains standing to this day. Originally it housed a board room and administrative offices plus facilities such as a gym, changing rooms and plunge baths. It meant players from either side could now prepare for games at the ground rather than the Talbot Hotel in Duke Street, a hostelry close to the centre of town from which they were transported to the ground by horse-drawn carriages. A tunnel led to the pitch with a move only taking place in the 1990s when the changing rooms were relocated to the Main Stand.

As part of a sponsorship deal, Knowsley Road spent the last two-and-a-half years of its life as St Helens RLFC's home referred to as the GPW Recruitment Stadium following a sponsorship deal announced in May 2008.

BATS AND BOTTLES –
THE NEW ST HELENS STADIUM

St Helens will move to a new stadium at some point in 2011 – even if the venue will not be ready for the start of Super League XVI. The 46-acre site is the long-derelict United Glass Bottles plant and a £25 million development to include not just the stadium but other amenities has been proposed since the early part of the millennium. However, the project has been beset by problems and while the credit crunch slowed construction down, this was just one in a line of hitches.

Demolition work began in January 2009 after planning problems which saw an eventual reference to central government for a final decision and a complication surrounding one of the old plant's kilns – Cannington Shaw No. 7 Bottle Shop to be precise. Though a dilapidated structure, its preservation and restoration was key to the go-ahead as the building, erected in 1886, is designated Grade II listed and an ancient monument by English Heritage. A plan was needed to ensure conservation to include the tunnels below. In addition, a colony of bats – who also enjoy protection – had made the kiln their home. These problems were eventually ironed out.

Though not exactly a home of rugby prior to Saints' arrival, 'UGB' did have a works side who played in the Challenge Cup. Ray French's father skippered the side just before the Second World War. Among others Jimmy Stott, a superb goalkicking centre, emerged from their ranks while working at the factory and went on to become a Saint.

ON THE ROAD

Like other Super League clubs, Saints have ceded home advantage at times to spread the gospel of Rugby League. An 'On the Road' concept was devised to showcase the new-look, and ultimately rebranded, sport under its new banner. This would be achieved by each club playing one game at a neutral venue, Liverpool Football Club's Anfield stadium has been used for games. The first was with Castleford in 1997 when, just ahead of the Challenge Cup final, more than 12,000 fans watched a comprehensive 42–16 Saints win. The following season the soccer ground was used again, this time for a game with Warrington, which Saints won 36–14. Although announced and accepted as a triumph, the idea was quickly abandoned. However, from 2006 Millennium and Murrayfield 'Magic Weekends' were created to take the game into Union heartlands. Essentially all clubs play a league match over a two-day festival close to the May Day holiday. Local derbies were first preferred until a draw based on the previous season's finishing positions was used. So far Cardiff and Edinburgh have had a couple of years each. A decision to move games from Scotland back to South Wales was made in 2010.

NATIONAL SERVICE

International teams have played at Knowsley Road as part of tours, with the ground also hosting encounters between other nations. England met Wales back in 1914 though it took more than a decade before another representative game was staged. This time it was England against Other Nationalities in 1930. France were the visitors in February 1939 for the final international played before the Second World War. England only returned in 1951 as hosts to Wales. Two years later the same venue saw England slay the Dragons by quite a heavy score. Great Britain met and defeated France in April 1957 and there were further cross-channel meetings in 1960, 1961, 1968 and 1971. England trounced Wales in May 1978.

St Helens was also one of the venues selected to host World Cup games in 1995 with New Zealand and Papua New Guinea doing battle. Five years later, England hammered minnows Russia 76–4 with Sean Long the only Saints man on a very extensive score sheet. The club last hosted a representative game in June 2006 when 8 St Helens players were in a Lions side which thrashed New Zealand. The new St Helens stadium is expected to get the nod to host matches in the 2013 World Cup.

ROUND BALL

Tom Finney is of course a name readily associated with football, but another Tom Finney was on Saints' books. The scrum-half's brother Jim was a soccer referee who would have officiated in the 1966 World Cup final if England had not reached the showpiece occasion. Another name those who know the round ball game will recognise is Emlyn Hughes whose father was a Welsh Rugby League international. His brother and uncle also turned professional though enjoyed less bountiful careers than Fred Hughes, or 'Ginger' as he was better known during his playing days. He made an appearance for Saints as a second-row forward in a War Emergency League game against Barrow – a club he served with some distinction.

Ted Forshaw had a career as a footballer until his mid-20s with Everton before joining the Saints and gaining half a dozen games as a mobile centre in the 1957/58 season scoring 3 tries and kicking 11 goals. He had failed to make the first team at Goodison Park and his rugby career also tailed off. But, being an innate sportsman he turned to athletics and eventually coached Pilkington Harriers plus a host of individual distance runners. There was an appointment as the Great Britain athletics team's manager during the 1980s.

Frank Brown not only switched rugby codes during the same season, joining Saints from the town's Union club, he also played soccer for St Helens Town. It is not unique for a person to play for the League, Union and Association Football clubs, although Brown is the only one to do so in the same season – 1947/48. His time at Knowsley Road was limited. After four first team games and a number of reserve outings over two campaigns he left.

HUNDREDS AND THOUSANDS

Saints became the first team to score more than 1,000 points in a season when leading the table at the close of 1958/59. The mark was reached and exceeded by another 5 points in the final game, a 15–14 defeat at Oldham. Tom van Vollenhoven's 53 tries during the regular season assisted that tally hugely and contributed to an overall total of 206 league touchdowns.

WAR GAMES

Though the league ran for a season during the First World War, the inevitable suspension of the professional game took place in September 1915. Friendlies from which newspapers (rather than the governing body) constructed merit tables, based on the same percentage system the Northern Union had adopted in deciding its league placings when points were tied, decided the table standings. The number of games played by each club was so unequal that there was little consistency until normal competition resumed in 1919. Saints had seen their resources severely depleted from the beginning of the war with 14 players volunteering to serve. Only Runcorn (with 21 men away) sent more of their number. The game's rules were tinkered with to accommodate the prevailing conditions which included government hostility to the sport. Twelve players were fielded rather than the usual thirteen due to severe shortage of available personnel. Three Saints men paid the ultimate sacrifice – Jimmy Flanagan, who served as a sergeant, was fatally wounded by shrapnel, and the centre who partnered him on the wing, Jimmy Greenwood, also died. Hubert 'Jum' Turthill, a London-born New Zealand international, also failed to return.

The attitude to sport was far more relaxed throughout the Second World War with a less stringent War Emergency League competition reinstituted. Saints hosted New Zealand just 24 hours before war was officially declared but measures were already afoot. Just over three weeks later games were back on, although initially restricted to a club's own side of the Pennines given the travel restrictions in place. There was also the sight of Union men being given permission to turnout in League games for the period of hostilities only. Sides representing each code also played a couple of matches to raise money for the Red Cross. Union rules were applied, though the Leaguers won each contest. Jimmy Stott, or Craftsman Stott as he was known due to service in the Army's Royal Electrical Mechanical Engineers, was the only Saints representative. The distinction between the lowly ranked League men such as Stott and officers who dominated the other code's representatives was notable. Along with Harry Pimblett, Stott also won England international honours as a Union man during the war years.

CLUB CLOSED

Though rugby continued during the First World War and provided many with a focus away from the conflict, St Helens only operated in the War Emergency League for two-and-a-half of the four-season break Northern Union games took. Having been defeated 22–0 by Widnes on 31 January 1918 the club simply closed its doors blaming a lack of finance for their decision. Only a few months earlier Warrington had paid the expenses of a very young Saints team to travel little more than 7 miles to fulfill a fixture at Wilderspool.

Players turned out for other clubs during what turned out to be an 11-month break when a friendly with St Helens Recs saw the doors reopened on Christmas Day. Saints were 'nilled' again with no answer to the 20 points put past them. Only three players who turned out against Widnes returned – Robert Heaton, John Holland and Herbert Hilton. When competitive football returned three weeks later, the Recs were faced again and although St Helens were well beaten once more, they did at least run a try in during the 24–3 defeat.

TOM BARTON – RELUCTANT TOURIST

When Tom Barton earned his sole England cap, the game being played at Wigan meant he didn't have to take much time away from work. Great Britain honours would have been added to that tally but for a refusal to join a tour of the Antipodes four years later. After being selected at half-back and attending a photo call with the travelling party, he opted out after the Northern Union refused to make up wages he contributed to his widowed mother. They only paid out the £1 compensation to dependent wives and would not bend the rules. Huddersfield's Jack Bartholomew, who has notoriety as the uncle of comic Eric Morecambe, took his place but missed each of the three successful Test matches against Australia and New Zealand after breaking his ribs in a warm-up game.

That gesture was typical of the man who as captain in 1915 managed to persuade his colleagues to turn out in the Challenge Cup final despite the disappointment of the team receiving no extra money for their achievement.

Barton reasoned that even a loser's medal was worth £3 – a princely sum – if anyone wanted to sell theirs. Tom was a winger with electric pace who covered 100 yards in 10.2 seconds when timed in championships held in Leigh during 1910. At that point he was 29 years of age. Just how fast he may have been earlier in his career is a fascinating question and made all the more intriguing by the fact he broke an ankle as a younger man and when it failed to heal, he went back to hospital to have the joint rebroken before undergoing more surgery.

As the initial operation implied, many procedures related to the bone did not always go well but without it Barton would have been forced to forget all about his sporting ambitions. He served the club for 17 years, utilising a superb kicking game and tactical acumen while acting at various stations in the backs and in official matches fell just three tries short of reaching a century. A confident goal-kicker he slung 118 efforts between the posts and had it not been for the First World War, would have become the first player to record 100 tries and 100 goals for the club. Unfortunately, none of his efforts in specially arranged competitions during the hostilities counted towards his career statistics.

JUST THE SAINTS

Unlike virtually every other Rugby League team – no matter what the standard of competition – St Helens have declined to adopt a nickname or addition to the club's original moniker. It is not a unique stance as others have carried the same epithets throughout their histories. Though in terms of those to currently have or once held Super League status, only Workington Town, who played in the debut campaign, stand apart with the Saints. Hull FC had four seasons as Hull Sharks and were initially known as plain Hull.

Very often names have carried through to the club's mascot which is usually a family-friendly touch in the sport. St Helens have been represented in those stakes with St Bernard and St Bernadette. When retired, the latter was replaced by Boots. Like his predecessors he is a St Bernard dog but somewhat stern-looking.

COACHING REGISTER

Since coaches rather than committees were given more responsibility towards team selection and player deals, St Helens have employed 19 men to take charge of on-field affairs. Alf Frodsham, Alan Prescott, Stan McCormick, Kel Coslett, Billy Benyon, Alex Murphy and Eric Hughes are the only ones to have both played for and coached the club. The most successful in terms of trophies alone is Jim Sullivan who, over seven years, guided the club to a debut Challenge Cup final win, two Championships, four Lancashire Leagues and a couple of Lancashire Cup triumphs. Daniel Anderson crammed a Grand Final win, four minor Premierships, three Challenge Cups and a World Club Challenge into just four seasons.

Alf Frodsham	1945–9
Peter Lyons	1949–52
Jim Sullivan	1952–9
Alan Prescott	1959–62
Stan McCormick	1962–4

Joe Coan	1964–7
Cliff Evans	1967–70
Jim Challinor	1970–4
Eric Ashton	1974–80
Kel Coslett	1980–2
Billy Benyon	1982–5
Alex Murphy	1985–90
Mike McClennan	1990–3
Eric Hughes	1994–6
Sean McRae	1996–8
Ellery Hanley	1998–2000
Ian Millward	2000–5
Daniel Anderson	2005–8
Mick Potter	2009–10
Royce Simmons	2010–

MILLION-POUND GAME

When St Helens met Halifax in the 1987 Challenge Cup final the 91,267 present generated more than £1 million in gate receipts, the first time seven figures had been earned from the sport's biggest game. Unfortunately, Saints fans were not the ones celebrating on the journey home. A John Pendlebury drop goal was the vital 1-point difference and the same player made a match-winning tackle on Mark Elia 8 minutes from time as the centre – who had already scored an excellent try and had another disallowed – seemed set to dive for a loose ball over the line. Despite looking second-favourite to reach it, Pendlebury got there first. Though decimalisation played its part in large increases of cash banked, Saints also played in the first £50,000 game when 98,536 generated just in excess of that amount in the Challenge Cup final, 21 May 1966.

PIONEER TOURS

In 1976 Saints became the first British team to tour Australia and New Zealand. There was an unofficial world title up for grabs should the newly crowned champions, who had also collected the Challenge Cup and Premiership Trophy, beat Aussie counterparts Eastern Suburbs. Friendlies took place against Queensland and an Auckland XIII as preparation. All three games ended in defeat with the match against Easts by far the heaviest. As a month had passed since the English season ended, match-sharpness had undoubtedly been lost. However, it wasn't just a shot at glory Saints were hoping for, nor a ground-breaking outlook towards the world. No, it was a much needed financial windfall as the series of games carried a guaranteed minimum of £9,000. Funds were seemingly endless Down Under while money was much tighter in the northern hemisphere.

PIMBLETT'S PREMIERSHIP POINTS RECORD

Across all Premiership finals, Geoff Pimblett has scored more goals and more points than any other player, his appearances in the 1976 and 1977 finals amassing 10 goals within an overall tally of 23 points. The remaining 3 came from a try scored in the win over Warrington in the latter of those two matches. Crossing the whitewash that day and landing 7 goals brought him 17 points – a record for a single Premiership match. Barrie Ledger shares the record for the most tries at 3 with a number of players.

MATCH RECORDS

In an individual match the various scoring records are:

Most points (40)	Paul Loughlin	v Carlisle	14 September 1986
Most tries (6)	Alf Ellaby	v Barrow	5 March 1932
	Steve Llewellyn	v Castleford	3 March 1956
		v Liverpool City	20 August 1956
	Tom van Vollenhoven	v Wakefield Trinity	21 December 1957
		v Blackpool Borough	23 April 1962
	Frank Myler	v Maryport	1 September 1969
	Shane Cooper	v Hull	17 February 1988
Most goals (16)	Paul Loughlin	v Carlisle	14 September 1986

Tom van Vollenhoven did score 7 tries in a friendly against the S.H.A.P.E. Indians, S.H.A.P.E. standing for Supreme Headquarters Allied Powers Europe – a team representing NATO military forces and featuring many continental players but mostly Americans working in the Paris headquarters. Coached by former US Navy American footballer Russell Mericle, they had played a match against the French Army and won but found a wider gulf in class against the Saints. The match took place at Knowsley Road on 7 May 1962. The winger added another couple of points by successfully sliding kicks between the posts.

Steve Llewellyn claims he could have bagged 9 tries against Castleford rather than the half dozen he officially scored but had three disallowed in the Challenge Cup second round 48–5 home win.

George Lewis kicked 13 goals in a Challenge Cup tie with Wardley on 16 February 1924. In the league Peter Fearis also notched a baker's dozen as Barrow were gunned down on 14 February 1959. For good measure he grabbed a try taking his total points to 29. Geoff Pimblett also put the ball between the posts 13 times in the league – against Bramley on 5 March 1981. He will have been disappointed not to have converted all 15 tries.

HEAVY WINNING MARGINS

A winning margin of 70 points or more has been recorded 8 times when a testimonial is included in such reckoning. The largest ever points difference after 80 minutes is the thumping 112 scored without reply against Carlisle in a Lancashire Cup opening round tie in September 1986. Three players – Barrie Ledger, Steve Halliwell and Neil Holding – grabbed hat-tricks. Only four of the starting line failed to register at least one of those points and the half-time score was a mere 32–0.

Ten players registered tries in another Lancashire Cup tie with Trafford Borough, Alan Hunte, Les Quirk and Anthony Sullivan each grabbing 3 of 16 touchdowns.

Saints are the only team to score a century of points in two competitive matches.

Margin	Score	Opposition	Date
112	112–0	v Carlisle (h)	14 September 1986
92	104–12	v Trafford Borough (h)	15 September 1991
80	80–0	v Warrington (h)	4 January 1996
75	75–0	v Wigan Warriors (h)	26 June 2005
74	78–4	v Leigh Centurions (a)	4 September 2005
73	73–0	v Wardley (a)	16 February 1924
72	84–12	v Mansfield Marksmen (h)	19 August 1984
70	72–2	v Warrington Wolves (h)	3 August 2002

HEAVY LOSING MARGINS

St Helens have lost by 70 points or more just twice, the worst defeat being a 78–6 thrashing at the hands of Warrington on 12 April 1909. The other occasion came during the Super League era when Leeds Rhinos put 70 unreplied points on the board against a Saints side which, although missing a few names, were capable of doing so much better at Headingley.

The record home defeat is a 65–12 mauling by Wigan Warriors on 26 May 1997. This time there was a higher number of significant names out, but the defeat was no less hurtful.

ONE SEASON OUTSIDE THE TOP FLIGHT

Over the various periods two or more divisions have been in operation, Saints have spent just one year outside the top flight – though there should have been at least one more. Placed in Division One after the Yorkshire and Lancashire leagues combined, they, along with Brighouse Rovers, were relegated at the close of the 1902/03 season. Bouncing back along with Wakefield Trinity the following campaign restored elite status although that too would have ended in relegation but for wholesale restructuring of the leagues into just a single competition, saving the club that ignominy.

MATCH SCORING RECORDS

David Traynor is the only Saint who has ever held the game's match record for the scoring of tries. His 5 against Lees in the Challenge Cup on 20 March 1897 shaded the previous mark. That same day two other players scored a nap hand elsewhere. Billy Jacques' eight goals, also against Lees, brought him the record for successful kicks in a single match. Adding a try landed him the then record points tally by any one player in a game. His total of 19 – just like his goals record – stood for just under two years. He did manage to grab both marks back for a while after leaving Knowsley Road and returning to the club he joined from – Hull.

ALF ELLABY – THE FIRST SUPERSTAR

Winger Alf Ellaby is genuinely the club's (if not the game's) first star, but he may well have enjoyed a career in Association rather than Rugby League Football save for a knee injury. The Scouser joined the club which became Rotherham United just months before he was forced to look at another trade. If it hadn't been for Ted Forber, who worked wonders with many St Helens Recs players, his employment would not have been as a professional sportsman and St Helens (let alone Ellaby) owed a large debt of gratitude to the trainer's skills. Not only was the problem sorted, the joint was strengthened allowing the winger to not only make consistent appearances (he missed only a handful of games over the course of the eight seasons which constituted his first stint at Knowsley Road), but withstand the knocks associated with being a winger.

More than a speed merchant, Alf's power was immense, although some felt he was much more reliant on that than ball or handling skills. Whatever the truth, he had far more than just the basic attributes as reflected by his scoring record – a first full season yielded 50 tries from 41 games. This was a ratio he would maintain until leaving the club. By the time he concluded his Saints career he had racked up 280 from 289 matches. Adding Lancashire, England and Great Britain into the equation plus the many times he crossed the line with Wigan, he set a record of 446 touchdowns which only a few other players, and none from the British Isles, have surpassed. In no small measure heavy scoring saw him dubbed the 'hat-trick king' and prior to Tom van Vollenhoven smashing the mark, Alf held the record for most tries in a season with 55. On the 1932 tour of Australia, Ellaby scored the quickest known try in Test history.

THE KIT BAG

Saints are noted for their distinctive red V on home shirts but the club began in vertical stripes of blue and white – a return to those colours was made in the centenary season of Rugby League in 1995. It was also the change strip for the inaugural Super League campaign.

Largely the colours sported have been red and white and prior to the V being introduced the white jersey carried a broad red band across the chest and the elbows of the sleeves. This dated from 1925 until 1961 when the red V was first introduced. The Challenge Cup was won with that pattern in 1961 and despite some returns to the red band plus a couple of tweaks of the basic V design – either thick, slender, fragmented, doubled, trebled or concentric – has remained ever since. A large plunging V and a chevron style have also featured. Sleeves have often been coloured rather than left white. There has also been all manner of geometric and other patterns adorning jerseys but the largest departure from the traditional design in recent years is the 1997 offering when the V was effectively white with a red and black diamond design around the bottom. It seemed more suited to leisure wear with denim jeans rather than something purely for on-field benefit.

Blue has been the dominant colour for change strips with various designs and shades. Black was an option in the early 2000s and green made an appearance as the decade neared its end.

FRENCH LESSONS

After more than a century of shunning professionalism, or at least officially doing so, Rugby Union's authorities accepted the concept in 1996 ushering in the prospect that players could switch from League to Union rather than just the opposite way. The open-door policy as it was known could also see players alternate between sports.

Until this point the two codes had been at nothing short of war. At its worst the disputes could be very bitter and often petty. Few people know that more than Ray French. Now a BBC commentator, he was a teacher who played Union with the St Helens RUFC. He made it to the England side in 1961, gaining four caps in that year's Five Nations. A switch of codes came soon after that series. After just over six seasons at Knowsley Road, Ray joined Widnes and gained more international honours. On hanging up his boots, French coached his old Union club as well as Cowley Hill School's sides. St Helens Rugby Union Club was born out of Cowley's old boys playing recreationally and on this news coming out, French was banned from coaching and even entering a clubhouse. However, they could not stop him having involvement with school rugby, given that he was employed as a teacher. Ironically French is now president of the Liverpool-St Helens RU club. His old team merged with their counterparts from up the East Lancs Road in 1986.

THOSE WHO WENT NORTH

Going north was the terminology for Welsh rugby players leaving the principality to join League ranks. Though there was always a steady stream of men willing to swap codes, the Northern Union had failed to flourish in the country. The WRU defended its patch well and were aided by their role in dishing out the playing fields available for sport. Any team that switched or even extended a hand to a League club risked having their ground taken away and with it their very existence. There was little money to acquire land and renovate it. There were moves to remedy this catch-22 scenario and Saints did what they could playing exhibitions in the late 1940s and 1950s. The game was appreciated but virtually all efforts made were in vain.

William Lewis, a right-sided centre, is reckoned to be the first player St Helens encouraged to break ranks. In 1896 (just over a year after the Northern Union was formed) he joined from Llanelli though his career only amounted to a couple of games plus a pre-season friendly. His try-scoring debut came in a match against Widnes when Saints were short-handed – only 14 men were available in what was still a 15-man game at the time. It is believed the prospect of being dropped caused him to have second thoughts about a professional career, though there is no record he ever tried to get back to Union.

A host of Union players have tested themselves with trial games, risking being spotted by Union scouts who might then report back to governing bodies who would hand out life bans. These players would appear on teamsheets as A. Trialist or A.N. Other. The practice was extremely widespread during times of economic depression though many left it at one game playing under a pseudonym.

Just after the Second World War George Parsons was threatened with suspension when the mere suspicion he had been approached was raised. He was actually kicked off a train headed for Paris when accusations were levelled following his resignation from Monmouthshire Police. His superintendent was a Pontypool official who simply passed on an unsubstantiated rumour. WRU secretary Walter Rees laid the accusations just as he boarded at Newport, departure was held up and as the train trundled away, Parsons was collecting his baggage telling journalists he had simply decided to leave the force and join the army rather than become a League player. The lock was a prized asset and while there was no evidence to suggest Saints were at the heart of any attempt to entice him, there were advances from the professional ranks. Parsons came to Knowsley Road in 1948.

Some switchers have proved to be among the greatest names in the club's history, Kel Coslett and John Mantle among others being prime examples. However, defecting did not always work out. Jim Webb, one of Union's best and most capped internationals, was a player who many thought was well suited to a forward's role in the Northern Union game. The former Abertillery man gained just five appearances within three months of his capture in October 1912. Despite a will to go professional after rows with the Welsh selectors and bags of ability, it simply didn't work out. Webb was also denied a chance to become a dual-code international when his Gloucester birthplace was revealed. Many said this should be ignored but Welsh officials were insistent. Soon after, Webb retired.

When Union did allow professionalism and became a richer sport able to reverse the previous trend, there was a hit-list of players who were offered handsome financial stimulus.

Anthony Sullivan was one to take up the offer and the schedules of each game allowing players an opportunity to play both codes simultaneously, was something the flying winger took full benefit from during his time at Cardiff Blues. Keiron Cunningham was headhunted but rejected the package put to him in 2001. The deal would have seen him become an exclusive Union player. Though no doubt tempted, when given 24 hours to make up his mind he has remained in the number nine jersey and saw out his 17th and final season in the autumn of 2010.

BRAVEHEARTS

Other than during the Northern Union's early years, Scottish players have been few and far between in Rugby League. As a nation they played their first recognised international in 1995. Those to have turned out for Scotland and been on Saints' books include Iain Marsh and Dave McConnell, who scored 4 tries in 5 games before deciding he had a better chance to make it by leaving Knowsley Road and dropping down the ranks in order to regain a chance in Super League. More notable members of Saints' Tartan Army include Castleford-born Paul Anderson who later turned out for England, and another Anglo is the country's leading try-scorer Danny Arnold. Lee Gilmour switched from England to Scotland while Australian-born Wayne McDonald (who captained the Scots) represented the United Arab Emirates in 2009 after emigrating to the Middle East state. McDonald is the only man to represent the nation while at St Helens. Phil Veivers is another Aussie who was able to turn out for the country though he gained his sole cap while with Huddersfield. Former Saints coach Shaun McRae had a five-match stint in charge.

IRISH HEARTS

Tim Jonkers, Chris Joynt, Tommy Martyn and Chris Maye all played for the Irish national side but none were born across the water – gaining their international recognition via a grandparent or other rules. Wiganer Joynt switched allegiance from England to the Emerald Isle but the others only played in green and white. Ian Pickavance and Joey Hayes were called into a squad during 1998 but failed to gain selection. After their time at Knowsley Road, Gary Connolly and Bernard Dwyer earned Irish caps.

FROM A LAND DOWN UNDER

Knowsley Road welcomed its first overseas player in 1908. The controversial but talented Kiwi Arthur Kelly had escaped charges of professionalism for taking a bet about his ability before fully embracing 'pay for play' by crossing to League and joining a lucrative tour which had stops in Britain. Kelly went home but swiftly returned after agreeing to join the Saints. Another player from that party to join him within the year was Herbert Turtill.

MISSING BUT IN ACTION

Albert Fildes and Alf Ellaby missed the 1932 Championship final and all other games from mid-April onwards after being required to make the lengthy sea journey to Australia with the Great Britain touring side. At that time the trek could take up to 76 days.

ALEX MURPHY – MURPHY'S LURE

In scenes that would have not seemed out of place in a spy novel Alex Murphy was signed almost as the clock struck midnight on his 16th birthday. Saints may have been expected to land the Thatto Heath-born scrum-half but his performances at schoolboy level were so impressive that there was no shortage of suitors. In fact after a turning out for his school's side in a final at Knowsley Road, four other clubs – possibly more – were said to have been waiting to speak to him and offer generous terms. It meant that the cloak-and-dagger tactics of getting him to the house of Joe Harrison, one of the club's directors, on Millbrook Lane and pushing the forms in front of his nose as soon as he was able to turn professional were more out of necessity than paranoia. After a quick meeting in the boardroom where the youngster (who had already trained with the first team) expressed his willingness to join, the board had simply decided they could not wait until the morning and allow those kicking their heels around the exit doors a chance to intercept young Alex.

However, just months later Murphy was demanding a transfer, frustrated that a handful of appearances for the 'A' team had failed to yield a shot in the senior side. His move denied, Alex was told he would be staying in the second string to learn his craft although a chance came when something of a reserve XIII was fielded against Whitehaven ahead of the 1956 Challenge Cup final. With Murphy pulling the strings among the backs he may have expected to be feted on the whistle – and would possibly deserved to it. Knowing Alex, he may have thought there was a chance of making the Wembley team but Jim Sullivan drew up a list of things which could have been done better plus some failings. Extra training was organised to sort out those flaws and add new skills to his natural flair. Murphy was determined that he would never have to listen to such a litany of errors again and put the work in. The result: a Great Britain international and the youngest ever tourist. Ultimately Alex became the world's greatest half-back of the early 1960s. A record was created with 27 tries from his first full season, being the best ever return from the scrum-half position. Like all young men in the late 1950s Murphy did National Service where he played Union for the RAF. A very competent fly-half and much coveted by the services he was denied a chance to join up with the Saints first team by a commanding officer who threatened him with a posting to Guam rather than just the routine square-bashing experienced in Britain if he maintained his demand for leave to travel. For once, and extremely begrudgingly, Murphy backed down.

A natural leader on the field, he was the obvious choice for skipper and took that responsibility from the 1962/63 season until leaving in 1966 after deciding he could not face being shifted out into the centres where he had spent the latter part of the season, while Tommy Bishop took the number 7 shirt. Challenge Cup and Championship final wins marking his last couple of appearances, he was excluded from training as well as the team when a transfer request was placed. There was no shortage of offers but a £12,000 fee put off those who were looking to land him. Leigh offered a coaching role which could be signed as long as he didn't play. That forced the hand of Aussie side North Sydney who promised a huge four-year deal and £8,000 for the Knowsley Road coffers. Leigh offered to stand aside but upped their stake to an unprecedented £30 per week. His first match in charge was a 29–5 win over an albeit injury-ravaged Saints. Twelve months later Leigh negotiated a £6,000 transfer to register Murphy as a player. It took almost two decades for him to return as a St Helens employee and this time as coach hoping to unseat one of the clubs he had guided since hanging up his boots – Wigan.

THEY SAID IT ...

'A lot of rubbish was talked at the time about what was best for the team. Murphy was the best player we had in any position – the greatest player you will ever see in your lifetime. Of course there was Vollenhoven – but he was a specialist. Alex was the complete footballer, a fine athlete and a tremendous trainer.'

Former coach Joe Coan reflecting on the decision to switch Alex Murphy – widely regarded as the world's best scrum-half – into the centres to accommodate Tommy Bishop in 1966.

'I am going to make St Helens the best club side in the World. It's Wigan at the moment, but we are going to take their place. The war starts now!'

Alex Murphy after his appointment as Saints coach in 1985.

THE ULTIMATE UTILITY MAN

Over 12 years Phil Veivers started games in nine different positions, but if you consider his substitute appearances as well, he has played in virtually every position on the field. From his preferred full-back position to front-row forward, the man often claimed to be a secondary part of the deal which brought Mal Meninga to Knowsley Road excelled in all disciplines. Far from an easy task, though, the Aussie should never be considered a basic utility man or jack of all trades. Nor should the great Kel Coslett who played in at least seven distinct roles.

LION'S ROAR

The first Saint to represent Great Britain did so in an up-country match used as preparation for Tests against Australia on the 1914 tour. However, it wasn't one of the club's stars or a player named within the touring party – it was the son of Joe Houghton (a Knowsley Road official who was managing the expedition) who gained selection as the Lions were three men short. Though he made up the numbers there was a bit of talent in the amateur who scored a try.

Les Fairclough became the first Saints player to play for and captain Great Britain. A debut came against New Zealand on home soil in 1926. By October 1929, when the Lions squared up against Australia at Craven Park, Hull, he had been named skipper. The tourists scored an easy 31–8 win.

SAINTS AGAINST THE WORLD

Touring international sides will often play club opponents as preparation for Tests. There have been some meek defeats against such outifts – especially from the antipodes – but also notable wins. These include a 9–0 defeat of the first Australian side to reach British shores in February 1909. A record 44–2 win was achieved against the same nation in November 1956 with an equally if not more impressive 37–10 win over Australia just a day after the Kangaroos were crowned World Champions in November 1970. Fatigue could be levelled as a reason but it is worth noting that Frank Myler and Cliff Watson played in both games for Great Britain and St Helens. The Aussies who played four ties spaced over almost three weeks also made changes but were simply outclassed. Alan Whittle had a superb game at scrum-half grabbing a hat-trick of tries. In 1952 and 1973 Saints were the only side other than Great Britain to beat the tourists, although the score was tight at 11–7 in the latter of those two encounters. No matches have taken place against Australia since 1994 and from 21 games, 8 have been won, 12 lost and 1 drawn.

Perhaps the most renowned victory remains the 1-point win over New Zealand in October 1989. Although there were well established names on show for the hosts, a number of injuries meant roughly half those on view were a scratch team. That showed at both the break and hour mark when the Kiwis held gaps of 7 then 11 points. In the twenty minutes which remained a dozen unanswered points completed an unlikely win. Saints have won 7 of the 15 meetings with the All Blacks who were last faced in October 2002.

French representative teams played two games within four days early in May 1953, and with the opener lost heavily,

Saints squeezed through the next encounter. Great Britain sides have been faced in warm-ups and testimonials and so too a GB XIII. St Helens remain unbeaten in these encounters but from elsewhere on the mainland Wales made testimonial opposition in 1975 and won narrowly. A Welsh side was faced on a trio of occasions in 1959 during a tour to promote the game and more latterly as a benefit match with three wins and a draw from four meetings. Italy failed to beat the Saints in the one attempt they have been afforded. Against combined international sides and those termed as Other Nationalities, who played officially sanctioned Test matches, Saints enjoy a mixed record with a defeat by an International XIII but a resounding victory over the Other Nationalities.

SOME WORDS FROM OUR SPONSORS

Company names were not allowed to be displayed on jerseys until 1985 and though St Helens Glass were the club's first sponsors, Saints headed to New Zealand with Pilkington emblazoned across their chests in 1985 for a quartet of games in a brief post-season tour. As may be expected, the glass manufacturers have been prominent among those agreeing deals with the club, most recently in 2008. St Helens Glass have had a couple of stints as the main shirt sponsor – initially that mid- to late 1980s period and then again in the early 2000s. McEwan's lager held a lengthy deal taking up most of the 1990s. They were replaced by John Smiths and Comodo, all:sports, Earth Money and Caledonia have followed suit. Earth Money and all:sports went bust while their deals were active. All manner of sponsors' names appear at various places on the shirts and shorts of rugby teams but concentrating on the main backer who will see their logos proudly reproduced across jerseys, Frontline Bathrooms have held the honour on home shirts since 2010 with Medicash taking the away strip.

The tie with Pilkington – one of the town's biggest ever employers – was a relationship extended at board level. Lady Mavis Pilkington acted as the club's president until her death in 1999.

Saints had hoped to incorporate a brand name on their jerseys well ahead of every club, bar Wigan. The great rivals were both denied the opportunity to allow logos on match shirts as early as March 1974. The fact games were carried on BBC television only was a huge factor given the corporation's attitudes to adverts of any nature – even kit manufacturers.

ALAN PRESCOTT – CAPTAIN COURAGEOUS

Aside from the acts of bravery carried out for his country, Alan Prescott served St Helens courageously over the course of 11½ seasons. He had gone through a couple of transformations prior to arriving at Knowsley Road via Widnes and Halifax at a cost of £2,000. The Yorkshire side blooded him before his 16th birthday. Starting as a winger he became a creative loose forward but a little more than a year after joining the club became a prop. Not the archetypal fit for the role, quite squat and standing a relatively short 5ft 10in, Prescott nevertheless turned in top class performances in that berth too. He was also a regular try-scorer due to the pace which helped him emerge as a junior.

Skipper of St Helens he also captained his county and Great Britain, leading each by example and deed. His influence was vital in Saints winning trophies from the mid-1950s until his retirement later in the decade. Chosen as coach in succession to a man who guided the club to so much glory, Jim Sullivan, Prescott was able to bring more silverware to the trophy cabinet but lasted only three years in the role – the theory being that he found the transition from pitch to sidelines far too difficult and wasn't quite the same task master he had been while on the field himself.

VINCE KARALIUS – WILD BULL

St Helens pipped Widnes to call on the services of giant teenage forward Vince Karalius. Despite some impressive performances when called upon, Ray Cale held the whip-hand for almost all the important games until the 1953/54 Lancashire Cup final against Wigan – there was no bigger match and the occasion was all the more important because of that. But even that first honour failed to help Vinty claim a place in the side. Four top quality players vying for the loose forward was a boost for the club, if not for those forced to wait their turn. Karalius's time as a first-team regular rather than squad member began in the mid-1950s though many of the games he did play were in the second row rather than in his preferred role. He was just as adept in such a demanding and tough role as the more creative aspects, and with various briefs assisted Saints to plunder a range of honours as the new decade approached. Just beyond that point he captained the club to more silverware including a Challenge Cup in 1961. Less than a year later, he joined his hometown club Widnes – with whom he also enjoyed Wembley victory.

A man for whom the term 'hard but fair' could have been invented, Vince was always appreciated by Saints supporters who also adored his bear-hug tackles. The mercurial Alex Murphy, who he often guarded against over-enthusiastic tacklers, was another fan. Murphy himself likened the situation to having one of the Kray twins looking after his interests. For a wider audience it was on Test rather than club duty that Karalius earned a nickname that would stay with him for a career. In 1958 an Australian journalist wrote of the Great Britain international as a dedicated wrecker of Aussie forwards – the Wild Bull of the Pampas. It was said to be a nickname Karalius didn't like – he thought of himself as considered rather than wild.

Always a fit man, Vince was often seen running between Widnes and St Helens but rumours that Karalius jumped from the Runcorn Bridge into the River Mersey are wholly false. Along with Alan Winstanley and Gordon Carney he dived into the Manchester Ship Canal – but only chose that body of water as the Mersey's tide was out! A section of the ship canal ran close to the river and was reachable with a decent dive from the same bridge. However, after each would-be Mersey diver hurt themselves they decided to abandon a future plan to jump, though Winstanley was said to have completed the task at a later date.

THEY SAID IT …

'He's the hardest player I have seen on a rugby field – and the nicest and most gentlemanly guy to meet off it.'
Alex Murphy on Vince Karalius.

KARALIUS CUP

The Karalius Cup, named after Vince Karalius, is contested between Saints and Widnes Vikings and worked into pre-season preparations. Karalius served both clubs with distinction and just weeks after his sad death in December 2008, the inaugural meeting was held at the Stobart Stadium. St Helens, who honour the fixture and their opponents by fielding a strong side, won impressively 54–6 and retained the trophy almost as emphatically in January 2010.

LEAPING FOR JOY

A Saints player who jumped canals was Pocket Nook's Matt Creevey. He took up the well-paid sport in the early 1900s and his leaping abilities were without parallel. Not only was he said to jump higher and further than anyone else could, he proved it and made money from his abilities. A world champion standing jumper he also performed in the highly popular music halls and anywhere else a crowd could be gathered. He vaulted clear over people from a standing position. Another trick was leaping over a couple of horses which stood 16 hands high without a run-up. Creevey would mount, then dismount in the same movement. He also soared above a double stack of chairs with a couple of tables laid at both ends and jumped backwards higher and further than anyone else could leap forwards. A handball player plus a super-fast runner with recorded times for the 100 yards (just over 10 seconds), Creevey had an equally impressive ability over longer distances. As a rugby player Matt used his pace and agility to good effect – mostly as a half-back playing more than 50 times at both scrum-half and stand-off where all his attributes would come into play. Two of his brothers – Charlie and Jimmy – played for the Saints. A third sibling, Luke, was a footballer but plied his trade elsewhere. Matt received a decoration from the Royal Humane Society when he rescued a woman from the Sankey Canal.

NULL AND VOID

A match with Salford in January 1926 won by a late try was declared void after appeals came from The Willows regarding Les Fairclough's touchdown, which they maintained included a double movement. On that same day John Logie Baird demonstrated his working model for the invention we now refer to as television – a useful tool administrators and officials now have the benefit of, but something not available to the RFL who upheld the complaint and expunged a 13–10 victory. The restaged game shunted to a Monday afternoon at the very end of the season was won far more easily. The line was crossed five times in the 23–0 win and none of the tries courted controversy. Gerald Barnes, who took over hooking duties, made his only appearance for the club in the game.

COSTLY BUSINESS

Although there have been concentrated pockets of investment by the Knowsley Road board, St Helens have not been noted for breaking the game's transfer records until very recent times. The first player to earn the accolade as a Saint was Stan McCormick who shattered the previous mark set by Ike Owens's quick flits from Leeds to Castleford and then Castleford on to Huddersfield, when changing hands at a cost of £4,000. Wingman McCormick was worth every penny paid to Belle Vue Rangers although it took the sale of Harry Street and Len Constance to raise most of the funds required. Another flanker, Mick Sullivan, came from Wigan with £11,000 a great persuader for the Central Park club. Effectively Jan Prinsloo made way and his sale to Wakefield Trinity raised just over 80 per cent of that huge outlay. Though his career didn't reach the same heights as it previously had, and his stay lasted three years, it is worth noting that Sullivan was utilised in a very different way. He played against and helped beat his old side in the Challenge Cup final. Intriguingly, the record he set was beaten soon after the deal went through – by £2 and 10 shillings.

Eric Prescott is the only Saints player to create a record when moving from Knowsley Road. The man who switched from a will-o'-the-wisp winger to a solid second-row forward attracted £13,000 when allowed to leave for Salford just after the 1972 Challenge Cup final. However, he played no part in the Wembley plans nor the Championship Final contested a week later.

TRANSFER SWAP SHOP

Transfers between clubs are virtually a thing of the past. Players under 24 years of age can still attract fees and there are provisions which allow an exchange of money. However, generally when someone wishes to leave a club or no longer features in a coach's plans they can leave under a freedom of contract on expiration of their deal, or simply by having their agreements cancelled. Even when transfers were very much a part of each club's business, straight cash wasn't always a method used to gain a player. Paul Newlove was valued at a world record £500,000 when joining from Bradford. Half that sum came in funds which the Yorkshire side could reinvest while three players - Bernard Dwyer, Paul Loughlin and Sonny Nickle – made up the balance.

DICK HUDDART –
NOW WASH YOUR HANDS

Whitehaven's first ever Great Britain international was eager to join St Helens; so keen in fact that he signed his contract using a toilet seat to lean the paper on. A desire to move from Cumbria was expressed soon after he completed his first stint of international duty – an Ashes-winning tour of Australia. Wigan had hoped to land the forward having gained permission and made a fair offer which Whitehaven accepted. But a friendship with Vince Karalius proved crucial in the player's own preference. Whitehaven had few qualms about taking £7,250 but were far from accommodating to the Knowsley Road contingent and offered them a lavatory to negotiate in, hence the practical use of that toilet seat.

At Whitehaven Huddart was known as 'the Tiger' due to the fact he tore opposing backlines to shreds. Most Marras players of the time rate the youngster as the best forward they had ever played with. Not just a strong man but a heavy scorer from the second row, Huddart was also a crowd favourite. Handing off was one of his talents and keeping the Cherry and Whites at arm's length probably ensured he would be well received at Knowsley Road. His whole-hearted performances and pacy ram-raiding of defences helped too. Over his first three seasons Huddart scored a more than creditable 48 tries and was a Lancashire Cup, Championship and Challenge Cup winner. Dick was handed the Lance Todd Trophy after that latter victory and deservedly so – in an excellent team performance his contributions were widely acclaimed as the most vital. He continued in the same vein for a few more seasons before the sporting respect he was held in by the Australians turned into a big-money offer to join St George. Everything had been won with St Helens and he continued in a similar vein with those other Saints replacing the great Norm Provan. A Grand Final win in 1966 meant Huddart became the first Briton to be so successful in Australia.

VISITORS FROM THE COLONIES

Bill Whiteley's testimonial in May 1910 came against something of a friendly foe, a side of 'colonial' players assembled by Jum Turthill. The visiting side scored an impressive 42–24 win.

WIGAN AND THE RECS

Wigan versus St Helens is the biggest clash in Rugby League, eagerly anticipated by fans of both sides and neutrals as the contests are usually so absorbing. They are typically exciting affairs too. Though not a derby in the true sense of the word it is considered as such by both teams.

St Helens Recs voted to join the Northern Rugby Union in June 1914 providing a genuine inter-town rivalry for the first and really only time. They remained at the ground Saints used before relocating to Knowsley Road a quarter of a century earlier – City Road. However, in straitened economic times a professional club simply could not be sustained, especially as the many Pilkington employees who boosted attendances gained free admission. Having found it impossible to remain in existence as a professional entity, the Recs folded after a game on 29 April 1939.

The sides enjoyed a keen rivalry in the years after the First World War until the Recs' financial collapse. St Helens lifted a first major honour against them at Warrington's Wilderspool ground in 1926 – Alf Ellaby and Les Fairclough had tries converted by George Lewis allowing skipper Fred Roffey to lift the Lancashire Cup. This was the only major final the sides contested although the Recs had lifted the same trophy three years earlier to steal a march on the town's senior Northern Union outfit. Most years the pair met on Christmas Day but their last game took place on New Year's Day 1939, with Saints winning 5–3.

Clashes with Wigan have traditionally been staged on Good Friday and Boxing Day. The change in calendar courtesy of the Super League era has left the Easter meeting intact, although the 1996 festive contest, brought back as the

Christmas Cracker or *Norweb Challenge*, was played over two legs for a £20,000 prize. Wigan had a young man called Sean Long at stand-off and both teams fielded youngsters so as not to risk their stars. Courtesy of a heavy win in the second game at Knowsley Road, Saints won 66–44 on aggregate having restored more of their bigger names. Twelve months on and a much less familiar side was put out with inevitable consequences. After a year out Wigan claimed victory at the JJB Stadium which given the facilities and ability to stave off bad weather staged the next contest in 2000. There were hopes of the match returning in 2009 but ice meant the Saints were unable to stage the contest and it remains retired.

A Christmas fixture has been contested almost annually since 1905 though it wasn't until 1967 that it became the key annual affair when both clubs – essentially meaning Wigan who were relegated at points in the 1970s and 1980s – were in the same division.

Consolidated record against Wigan:

	P	W	D	L	Pts F	Pts A
League	221	84	10	127	2913	3708
Play-offs/ Championship	10	5	0	5	205	205
Premiership	11	6	1	4	173	217
Challenge Cup	26	9	3	14	288	356
JPS/Regal Trophy	3	0	0	3	43	58
Lancashire Cup	19	6	0	13	208	298
Floodlit Trophy	6	1	2	3	60	68
Yorkshire Cup	4	1	0	3	51	74
Wartime games	19	3	1	15	115	236
Friendlies	13	5	0	8	196	291
Total	**332**	**120**	**17**	**195**	**4252**	**5511**

Biggest victory:
75–0   26 June 2006   Challenge Cup   Knowsley Road

Biggest defeat:
58–4   26 December 1995   League   Central Park

Matches against both Wigan and Pilkington Recs, who were formed from the old St Helens Recs club, took place as part of the Queen's Silver Jubilee celebrations in August 1977. Within 72 hours Saints beat both at Knowsley Road, the amateurs pushing them closest for the win.

DOWNING TOOLS

A far from unexpected defeat to Wigan came in the opening round of the 1976/77 Lancashire Cup when almost the entire first team took strike action over a pay dispute. Some who would never represent the first team again pulled on a jersey at Central Park with one national paper suggesting a team of 'little green men' could not have looked any stranger than this St Helens side. Only seven had any first-team experience with 19-year-old Harry Pinner making his 13th senior appearance the only recognised current first choice. The line-up was so scratch in nature there was even a need to play a couple of trialists plus an amateur. Winger Raymond Howarth, who got his only senior start outside a friendly, was the eldest at 31. The second string fought gamely but were powerless to stop Green Vigo who scored 7 tries and equalled the host team's match record. Pinner struck a penalty with Mike Hope touching down to claim the 3 additional points scored. Partly due to the spectacle, only 2,370 paid to gain entry – the lowest derby crowd at either Knowsley Road or Central Park since 1901.

GOING DUTCH

Tom van Vollenhoven and Errol van Niekirk (among others) may have Dutch sounding names, but given that their home nation, South Africa, saw plenty of settlers from Holland make their home there since the late 1800s it is understandable. Tim Jonkers is the only player from the Netherlands to wear a Saints shirt. Born in Amsterdam his family relocated to St Helens in the late 1980s when Tim was 6. Fully embracing the town and its culture he joined the Blackbrook club. Signed by Saints as a highly promising 17-year-old forward, Jonkers made his debut while still at school. He realised plenty of early potential until he was struck by knee injuries and allowed to leave. Link-ups with former coaches – Shaun McCrae (Salford City Reds) and Ian Millward (Wigan Warriors) – showed there remained much belief in Jonkers, but a recurrence of his old problem and new niggles linked to that damage meant he retired just before his 26th birthday. Rather than represent Holland, which had no national team until 2005, or England as he was also qualified to do and had at under-21 level, Tim played international rugby for Ireland courtesy of the grandparent rule.

A BETTER PLAYER THAN VAN VOLLENHOVEN?

Alex Murphy earned his wages outside rugby as a joiner with St Helens Council. As an apprentice he worked under Bill Mercer, a great centre of the late 1920s and early '30s who captained the side and also served as a trainer to the 'A' team. On learning that Tom van Vollenhoven received pay from the Saints over the close season – virtually unheard of in Rugby League – Murphy asked for a similar privilege. The request was dismissed and the scrum-half was told he was not as good a player as the flying South African wingman. Murphy retorted that he was in the summer.

ALIAS SMITH AND JONES

The United Kingdom's most common surnames remain Smith, with 1.22 per cent of the population holding that family name, and Jones, estimated to be shared by 0.93 per cent of people according to surveys in 2008. Players with the surname Smith or Jones are in equal number on the club's books with 22 of each.

ARMY RATIONS

The British Army made their Challenge Cup debut in 2008 and participate in a number of amateur competitions. Coached by St Helens-born Sergeant Sean Fanning, they met Thatto Heath in the first round proper where the Crusaders were able to field a liberal sprinkling of Knowsley Road academy players. Saints played an Army team during the Second World War winning 6–3 on 13 February 1943 at home. During the First World War a match took place on 3 March 1917 against the South Lancashire Regiment who drew their ranks primarily from the town plus Warrington. Saints won 33–5.

A COMPLETE HEAD THE BALL

Towering prop John Harrison has a rare distinction in Rugby League. He is the only player to head a ball during a set of six. The innovation came on the fifth tackle in a home game with Sheffield Eagles during November 1990. Saints were just yards out but the line seemed well patrolled until Harrison simply nodded the ball on allowing George Mann to scamper through and touchdown. The visitors were not sure how to react until the points were awarded. It was a move worked on at the training ground by coach Mike McClennan who had a liking for the unorthodox and once played for the delightfully named Ponsonby Ponies.

LONG-DISTANCE KICKING

Although players have become progressively stronger and far more adept at kicking goals, successful attempts from over halfway remain rare. Len Killeen made what is still said to be the best, let alone longest, kick in Wembley history just ten minutes into the 1966 Challenge Cup final with Wigan. The South African rarely missed, and even difficult efforts became something of a regulation strike on his toes. However, not even Len was expected to find the target in the national stadium's febrile atmosphere from 65 yards, especially at such a nervy time. He had already steered one home from less then half that distance but close to the touchline Killeen sought to and successfully doubled that early advantage. With Wigan struggling in a highly tactical battle it went some way to breaking their resolve.

The longest distance kick ever landed between the posts in the game's history was at Knowsley Road but the feat was not performed by a Saints player. It was Castleford's Arthur Atkinson in a league match on 26 October 1929 during the process of scoring a penalty in a 20–10 win for the visitors. His huge 75 yard (or 68.5 metre) effort was perhaps better described as gale- rather than wind-assisted.

LONG-DISTANCE RUNNING

Len Killeen is also the scorer of the longest ever try recorded at Knowsley Road. During the closing minutes of a game with Warrington on 7 November 1964 he took a kick from Geoff Bootle behind his own try line. Getting to the other end of the field would not have been on many players' minds, but after seeing a chasm ahead due to some lax defending by the charging winger and his centre, Killeen hared to the posts. The backline broken, there was now nothing but clear space ahead. Only Parry Gordon looked capable of catching him but the scrum-half only got within a few yards, doing no more than causing the centre to veer right. Len finished with 6 goals in the 26–10 win. He would have bettered the tally by one had he not been so tired that converting his try proved impossible. He spent much of the time following the touchdown recovering in the goal area. As Alex Murphy landed the extras, Killeen was steadily trotting back down the field's perimeter. The total run was later measured at 100 yards.

LOSING HIS DEPOSIT

Mick Murphy, a 17-stone prop who could dash 100 metres in an extremely impressive 11 seconds, made a shade fewer than 100 appearances for the club before joining Bradford Northern. On leaving the game he turned his hand to acting with minor roles in *Emmerdale* and *A Touch of Frost* before adding another string to his bow as a would-be politician. He joined and left the St Helens South Labour Party in the space of a week during May 2001 to protest against the candidature of Shaun Woodward. Murphy, who stood as an independent, suggested Woodward had been parachuted into the safe seat for that year's General Election after defecting from the Conservatives. His old constituency of Witney – the seat inherited by David Cameron – in its many guises had never elected anyone standing under anything but the Tory banner. Although Labour's share of the poll was down, only a tiny amount of that was down to Murphy who garnered just 271 votes. Murphy now lives mainly in Southern France, a part of the world he knows well after serving St Jacques and Tonneins.

LEN KILLEEN – LENNY THE LION

Another exceptional talent in a long line of goal-kicking wingers, Len Killeen spent much of the 1960s plying his trade with St Helens before heading Down Under to become the first South African to win a Grand Final there with Balmain Tigers. Weighing in with a try almost every game in his first season at Knowsley Road, his contribution dipped for a campaign, though was back up again with his overall points collection greatly enhanced by a responsibility now being taken for a shy at the posts. This period coincided with the most glorious part of the club's post-war history – at least until that point – and the 1965/66 four-trophy haul. All the points in a Challenge Cup semi-final win over Dewsbury were scored by Killeen who also made a huge contribution in the showpiece, winning the Lance Todd trophy as a result.

He had achieved all he could in the northern hemisphere so the challenge that Killeen took when leaving the club in 1967 was perhaps understandable. St Helens received £4,500. He maintained his prolific record hitting 664 points in the 78 games played over five seasons and is feted whenever he returns to Balmain. Many of the records he set there still remain intact and the club haven't won the Premiership since his exploits in 1969. Aside from his rugby skills Killeen was a very good cricketer, played baseball to a high standard and represented his country at basketball.

SEASON'S BESTS

Most points	Kel Coslett	452	1971/72
Most tries	Tom van Vollenhoven	62	1958/59
Most goals	Kel Coslett	214	1971/72

Austin Rhodes fell just a tantalising point short of becoming the first Saint to reach the 400 mark in a single campaign at the close of the 1959/60 season, no doubt replaying any chances he missed after the final game. Other than Coslett, Paul Loughlin is the sole player to hit a quadruple century or more, bagging 424 points in the 1986/87 season. Tom van Vollenhoven bettered a half-century of tries twice and Alf

Ellaby is the only other player to post more than 50 in a season. In 1986/87 Loughlin came within 10 goals of becoming only the fourth player to hit 200 goals or more. Coslett was 7 shy of reaching a double century a season before, finally becoming just one of three players to achieve the feat.

Various players have finished as the league's top scorer in terms of tries, goals or overall points, but a Saint has seldom topped each chart in the same season. The first came in 1960/61 when van Vollenhoven finished top of the try-scoring charts with Rhodes top goal-kicker and points scorer. The second and last occasion was in 1996 when Paul Newlove was top try-scorer with Bobbie Goulding the heaviest goal-getter and points scorer. Len Killeen topped all three categories in 1965/66 and remains the only player to do so.

CHAMPIONS

Including titles decided by Premierships and Grand Finals St Helens have won 16 championships: 1931/32, 1952/53, 1958/59, 1965/66, 1969/70, 1970/71, 1974/75, 1975/76, 1976/77, 1984/85, 1992/93, 1996, 1999, 2000, 2002 and 2006.

Minor Premierships and League Leaders' Shields – when leading the table did not decide the championship – have been collected on 13 occasions. In eras when clubs were unable to call themselves champions despite finishing top, St Helens have still have held pole position and had the honour of being crowned champions by virtue of winning the play-offs in 1952/53, 1958/59, 1965/66, 2002 and 2006. St Helens have won championship deciders when not top in 1931/32,

1969/70, 1970/71, 1999 and 2000. Only one of these titles came from a position lower than runners-up – Saints came through after finishing third in the 1969/70 table.

FAIR PLAY TO THE SAINTS

Fair play in the game is measured by a system of points related to all manner of fouls and penalties conceded. Those who amass the lowest tally receive a small cash prize from the sponsors. In 2008 Saints picked up £5,000 for limiting themselves to just 222 points from 27 Super League games.

TOM VAN VOLLENHOVEN – A BOY FROM BETHLEHEM

All manner of precious minerals and metals have been hewn from the earth of South Africa and St Helens found a gem in the shape of Karel Thomas van Vollenhoven – better known as Tom. With the new acquisition reigning South African Sportsman of the year it may seem the club was always on to a winner. It was well known that the wingman had many admirers in both codes but with communications between countries limited and very few reports or live telecasts of rugby games around the world, the Northern Transvaal's flanker remained something of an unknown quantity to those he would be playing with at Knowsley Road. They knew he must be good, but possibly not how good, nor how fast. Van Vollenhoven was so quick it was outrageous. Strangely he only took to the flanks after being asked to cover the sprints in schools athletics. A decent middle-distance man, he completed the 100 yards in a mere 10.5 seconds. He got faster as his muscles and strength developed. His pace shocked his new team-mates when the South African first attended a training session.

Not only that, despite being whip thin he was strong enough to hold off a range of challenges and make vital tackles. Often an opposing flanker – no matter which side of the field he was on – would hear Tom thundering after him then be hauled down. Few knew he was a forward in his teens and then a centre. However, when unleashed in matches (including his debut in late October 1957 against Leeds) a very well-kept secret was certainly out. That appearance, like so many of the 408 which followed, was a scoring one. However, there was a lapse which allowed the Yorkshire side to grab a try. Not bad for someone who was so poorly with a childhood chest problem that he did very little sport and was kept away from any athletic activity involving heavy contact.

His second season saw him claim a club record for the most number of tries in a single campaign and his use in a side focused on good attacking football was a major factor in Saints enjoying huge success in the 1960s – the club's most triumphant decade until the Super League era dawned. Only injury, which was an inevitable risk as defenders would often do anything to stop him (including skullduggery), ever saw his try return reduce below 20 for a season. Even when carrying a knock 'Vol' was a man to be feared. Despite not being fit due to a hamstring problem, the winger grabbed 3 tries in the 1959 Championship final win over Hunslet including a solo effort which took him almost the entire length of the pitch and past half a dozen players. Only once was he benched and that was for a tour match with New Zealand. He finished with 392 tries from 408 outings. His last season coincided with his testimonial year and to underline his popularity a record £2,800 was raised. A final game on English soil did not come in a Saints jersey, however – it was as a guest for Great Britain's 1968 World Cup team in a warm-up with Halifax. Tom signed off with a hat-trick of tries.

PUNCTURED BICYCLE
LEFT WIGAN DESOLATE

When Tom van Vollenhoven decided he was open to approaches from Rugby League clubs there was no shortage of offers. He would have been a Warrington player if all had gone smoothly when he first looked at leaving South Africa. International cricketer George Duckworth, who played more than 500 games for Lancashire as a wicket-keeper and batsman, approached him about joining the Wire when on tour with the MCC in 1956. Others ran the rule over him, though St Helens and Wigan were perhaps always the front runners and were certainly prepared to make handsome offers. Wigan tendered £2,000 but that failed to do the trick. Central Park chairman Bill Gore took a plane out to present an improved proposition in person. There was hope that van Vollenhoven would complete a devastating threat down each wing in tandem with Billy Boston.

St Helens got a school teacher based 300 miles from van Vollenhoven's Pretoria home to act as their agent in negotiations. To add insult to no small measure of injury felt at Central Park, the man chosen was not only a born and bred Wiganer but more than happy to take the role.

Realising Gore would not beat his rival to the punch, a telegram was dispatched to the player's home promising to top any offer St Helens made. Legend has it that Saints managed to get their £4,000 proposal in his hands first and that Wigan's message boy was delayed when suffering a puncture on his bicycle and had to repair it. The Knowsley Road man completed his journey and had an agreement signed just a matter of minutes before the youngster managed to reach what was his last delivery of the day.

CHAMPIONSHIP FINAL HEROICS

Tom van Vollenhoven grabbed 3 tries in a Championship Final as did Albert Halsall, in 1959 and 1966 respectively. Len Killeen holds a share of that record grabbing a hat-trick in the heavy win over Halifax in that latter game but courtesy of a fine all-round display holds the total points record with 21. Austin Rhodes recorded the most goals – 10 – in the 1959 final.

FIRST FROM THE BENCH

Ray French was the first player to be called from the substitutes bench after replacements were allowed to be named in the 1964/65 season. David Harvey, the other substitute named on the day, was also brought into the action. Replacements could only be pitched in for injured colleagues and even then such changes were limited to the opening half. Billy Benyon and Stan Owen who represented two very different ends of the age scale were named as replacements in a friendly with Swinton eight days earlier. Though both were used and were in the truest sense the first substitutes deployed officially, French takes the distinction.

Though a substitute can see much of the game under today's rules, just three replacement players have grabbed a hat-trick of tries – Anthony Sullivan v Trafford Borough in September 1991, Mickey Higham v London Broncos in May 2003 and Mark Edmondson v Wigan Warriors in June 2005.

IN THE FAMILY WAY

Often referred to as the family game due to the profile of fans attending games and spirit among supporters, it should be noted that there are plenty of family ties across the field as well as in the stands. Twenty-one sets of fathers and sons have been on the club's books.

Three generations of the Arkwright family have had stints at Knowsley Road and made the first team. Jack Arkwright was one of the club's first stars though his son John only had a short spell in the first team comprising of 14 games over the early part of the 1962/63 season. Grandson Chris played almost 300 matches and was named skipper in the 1980s.

Though there are probably more, given that squads stretch back to a number of ranks and the records most clubs hold are scant in their early years, 39 sets of brothers seem to have plied their trade with the Saints. Outside those closer family ties, Harry and James Greenwood were cousins, Mike Bennett is the great-great-nephew of Harold Heaton, Chris Maye referred to Chris Joynt as 'Uncle Chris', and Harry Pinner is William Fishwick's nephew.

Brothers have faced each other in a Challenge Cup final involving St Helens – Paul and Danny Sculthorpe with Saints and Wigan Warriors respectively in 2004. Two years later Ade Gardner hoped to match up against his younger sibling Mat who, also a winger, was part of the Huddersfield Giants squad but failed to make the 17 at Twickenham.

PAUL WELLENS – MR ST HELENS

Though a hugely versatile performer who has played on the wing, both centre berths, scrum-half and even hooker, Paul Wellens is without doubt the finest full-back of the modern era. More than ten years of service to the first team and far more when his junior days are taken into account make the moniker 'Mr St Helens' a very apt reference. His role is by definition defensive and should an attack manage to break through the usually well-drilled ranks, the ball carrier always has one eye searching for Wellens and there are few better exponents of defusing the high bomb kicks many half-backs look to pepper the try line with. Wellens is a safe pair of hands no matter what trajectory or arc the ball has. Errors over an entire season let alone a single game can be counted on the fingers of just one hand. His ability to make yards when fielding the ball deep in his own territory and twist over the try-line when seemingly penned in is widely renowned. As and when required he also makes the odd kick for goal. A ghosting presence in attack he is well on the way to a double century of tries and has provided countless lay-offs. All these qualities saw him named as 2006 Man of Steel and a worthy recipient of awards from both his peers and those in the press box. He concluded that same campaign as the Harry Sunderland Trophy winner. England and Great Britain honours were a matter of course. Rarely injured, in theory he could serve at least another half decade before finally calling it a day. Even when he does encounter a fitness problem, Paul will usually attempt to play through it, as witnessed by the fractured eye socket sustained after just two minutes of the 2002 Grand Final. At the final whistle his clenched-fist salute of the win evoked comparisons with the conclusion of *Rocky* films.

LEADERS ALL THE WAY

Saints hit top spot after the first game of the 2006 Super League season and retained it until the season ended 27 games later. A 24-point win over Harlequins matched Hull FC's win over Castleford but when the pair won the following week – St Helens mauling the Tigers at the Jungle – they improved a points difference over the Humberside outfit by 10. Hull, who finished a distant second, eventually dropped away – especially after Saints cruised to a 46–0 win at the KC Stadium. The Black and Whites gained retribution with victory by the odd point at Knowsley Road, one of just four games Saints lost that term. In addition to that slim loss was a 2-point defeat to Bradford Bulls, a defeat by 3 points to Huddersfield Giants and a 4-point deficit against the Catalans Dragons. All those games could have gone the other way and been won.

THROUGH THE PAIN BARRIER

When Great Britain's players spent much of the week they had to prepare for a second of three Tests against Australia on the 1958 tour in Surfers' Paradise, many wondered just how serious they were taking the task ahead of them – especially after a thrashing in the opening game. However, those doubters could not have been wider of the mark. The series was tied with Alan Prescott playing 77 minutes with a broken arm. He shattered the bone in an uncompromising, early – though legal – tackle on Aussie back-row forward Rex Mossop. Prescott realised the damage was bad; he also knew the prognosis and implications. His right-hand side virtually useless, he played the ball and went into scrums on the opposite side to protect the limb as best he could but knew he was a huge target for those in green and gold. There were no substitutes to call on at the time. That innovation was some six years off so the only choice was to carry on or go off.

The team doctor insisted the captain should choose the latter option and although an Australian, there was no question of the opinion being anything other than medically driven. Prescott ignored that advice to not only carry on but direct play in a 25–18 win in Brisbane. The skipper spent just half a minute in back play having the arm bandaged. Debutant Vince Karalius thought his game was over at half time due to a back problem which not only impaired a performance which had been devastating until that point, but stopped him walking. However, after being coaxed to his feet and helped towards the field, he managed to complete the game. He also played a full part in a remarkable win having been switched to stand-off from the pack to cover for Dave Bolton who having broken a collar-bone had to accept the inevitable. Including Prescott and Karalius, five men needed hospital treatment after the game. Four players all but incapacitated and a man down, the Lions roared harder in the second period. Karalius set up vital tries for Ike Southward and Alex Murphy. On the same tour four years later Murphy played an entire warm-up match against St George with an arm injury. It was later discovered to have been a break.

HELD TO NIL

As Rugby League is a sport with generous points-scoring opportunities, 'nilling' a team (stopping a side from scoring) can be a rarity. It is even less common to nil a team twice in the same season. Saints have achieved the feat just a handful of times and a mark of how seldom it occurs is gained by the 55-year wait between both Liverpool City and Swinton not being a allowed to register a point during the 1953/54 season and the next occasion it happened, against Super League new boys Celtic Crusaders in 2009.

CAREER BESTS

The highest tallies for points and scoring in a Saints jersey are as follows:

Most points	Kel Coslett	3,413
Most tries	Tom van Vollenhoven	392
Most goals	Kel Coslett	1,639
Most drop goals	Harry Pinner	73

HARRY PINNER – ACE IN THE PACK

A man who would have graced the game in any period, Harry Pinner was identified as a rare talent in his teens and before hitting 20 had not only broken into the first team but looked totally at home in top-grade rugby. In fact he was already being identified as not just a force for the future, he was already guiding far more experienced colleagues. At the tail end of his distinguished career he was conducting a band of promising youngsters with the same virtuoso flair. Every try and virtually each move had Pinner's fingerprints somewhere in it. With hand or via the boot, Harry saw many things others could not – especially the opposition. Though he missed out on a Wembley appearance in the 1976 Challenge Cup there was a part to play from the bench in the Premiership Final. For over 300 games after that win Harry was a fixture in the side and the best loose forward on view.

Over his career he was keen to drop goals, and not just for grabbing wins by the odd point or to ensure teams had to score at least twice in tight games; Pinner used it as a method to apply pressure and turn the tide of a particular encounter. A drive towards the posts yielding any kind of reward would see the ball kicked straight back to the Saints and careful husbandry up the pitch would as often as not bring a try courtesy of a ball-running charge.

A switch to Widnes was arranged when Alex Murphy wanted to land John Fieldhouse for the pack. Neither player flourished in their new surroundings. Fieldhouse left for Oldham and had many other stops before briefly heading back to Naughton Park. Pinner spent two seasons with the Chemics making relatively ad hoc outings prior to hanging up his boots and becoming a very popular publican.

TOP TEN APPEARANCES

Kel Coslett	430 (18)
Billy Benyon	438 (11)
William Briers	509
Eric Chisnall	425 (30)
Keiron Cunningham	467 (28)
Douglas Greenall	481
George Lewis	423
Tom van Vollenhoven	404
Les Jones	394 (9)
John Mantle	337 (13)

Numbers in brackets indicate substitute appearances.

The demanding nature of Rugby League and distinct positions means very few players reach a century of consecutive appearances. The best any Saint can muster over the past 115 years is the 87 Chris Joynt managed to string together between April 1999 and June 2001. Joynt broke a record Harold Smith had held for 72 years when lining up against Hull in a Super League match at the KC Stadium. The captain missed the next game.

BILLY BENYON – ONE-ARMED BANDIT

As a teenager Billy Benyon had a very real choice between soccer and Rugby League. A couple of professional clubs were willing to offer him terms in the round ball sport but as a good St Helens lad he chose the Saints and rugby. He had little reason to regret that decision and those skills with his feet often came in handy. As a centre there were opportunities to send in low kicks to stretch defences and play in the wingers among others. Len Killeen had few reasons to question the tactic as quickness of mind was mirrored by a quickness on his feet. That too opened doors for others but at some stages Billy himself was able to exploit his own work and cross the whitewash, never more so than in the 1969/70 and 1970/71 campaigns when he scored 22 tries in each season.

Even when something of an old stager, Benyon barely slowed and the trophies kept coming. How cruel that the man who was the club's most decorated player with 16 medals from 20 finals lifted just one trophy as skipper. He took the role when Kel Coslett left in 1976 but only got his hands on the Premiership trophy at the end of his first season as captain. His second and last term saw defeat in the BBC TV Trophy and Challenge Cup finals. The latter was especially disappointing as Saints surrendered a decent lead courtesy of being out-muscled by the Leeds forwards after the restart. A move to Warrington was brokered soon after that second frustrating defeat. At Wilderspool he claimed the only medal missing from his collection – the John Player Special Trophy. There was a return to St Helens in 1982 and a second succession to Coslett, this time as coach. Three and a bit seasons in charge yielded a team of youthful promise graduating to fully fledged seniors with two more pieces of silverware, the first successes since his playing days and the end of a seven-year drought for the club.

AN EARLY PIONEER

Salfordian James Peters was, like all his family, a circus performer. His days in the Big Top started as child horse rider. His brother was a clown and father a lion tamer (until he was killed while in the cage training his animals). The early 1900s were extremely hard for those of West Indian extraction such as the Peters family who, having lost their largest wage-earner, were forced into measures which included sending young James away and sadly abandoning him. He proved to be an excellent schoolboy sportsman playing cricket and rugby plus excelling as an all-round athlete across distances and disciplines. Initially a printer he retained his involvement with rugby if no other sports playing for Knowle in Bristol. Unfortunately some members objected to his colour and resigned. There was only a slightly better reception on playing fields in Plymouth where he also worked as a carpenter in the Devonport Dockyards. While turning out for the county, South African tourists refused to play a game on seeing Peters.

England selectors picked him for a match with Scotland in March 1907 when he became the first black person to represent his country. Again, racial bigotry became a factor in much of the analysis. After scoring against France in the next Test he was left out against the Springboks – at their request – though came straight back into the side against the home nations. The loss of three fingers in a work accident failed to impair his performances but taking money to play from clubs seeking to introduce professionalism in the South West left him no choice but to try League. After the best part of a season with Barrow he joined St Helens but at 35 years of age was never going to stay long and played just two games within a week at scrum-half. Not long after, he retired. A resident of the London Borough of Greenwich while an orphan, he is so highly regarded and celebrated as a sporting pioneer that Greenwich Admirals ARL play an annual match in his honour.

FRANK WILSON – AN UNENVIABLE TASK

As if switching codes and moving from South Wales to Lancashire was not a sufficient enough transformation of Frank Wilson's career, he was also charged with the duty of taking over from Tom van Vollenhoven. The winger had attracted much interest from professional clubs though the most prominent, Wigan, failed to follow up their enquiries and were made to pay a heavy price. St Helens' top try-getter in his first season and a number of others which followed, Wilson may not always have been a heavy scorer in games but his contributions were frequent with tries virtually week in week out. However, it was the manner in which he crossed the whitewash which impressed as much as the regularity. He had great pace – but that would be expected for his position – which aligned with his speed of thought, balance, agility and strength meant he made an impact in both attack and defence. Comfortable on either flank, he had lengthy spells both left and right. When Ray Mathias was also brought north, Frank switched into the centre forming a devastating partnership with Les Jones.

Towards the end of his time as a Saint there were run outs at stand-off, although his final game in a red V – a friendly with Auckland – plus a few more in the spring of 1976 were back as a wingman. If there were disappointments in a career spanning more than 300 games and well over 500 points it was missing out on medals due to the tactical whims of coaches or injury. But given his time at Knowsley Road coincided with one of the club's most productive in terms of silverware, there was still plenty of metal on display in addition to Welsh caps. After serving Workington Town, Warrington and Salford there was a chance for Wilson to see out his career back in his home city with the re-formed Cardiff City in the Second Division.

THERE IS POWER IN A UNION

In one of their most unusual friendly games, St Helens beat a XIII representing the Players' Union in an end of season match held during late April 1951. Approximately 4,000 spectators witnessed a 45–38 home win at Knowsley Road.

THEY SAID IT ...

'I'd rather be on Blackpool beach than Bondi beach. They can keep the country to themselves.'

Leon Pryce at his diplomatic best on Lions duty Down Under.

VEGAS STRIP

Weighing in at 18 stones Thatto Heath's Michael Pennington made just one appearance in a Saints jersey. But as the match was Keiron Cunningham's testimonial, the outing which lasted just a few minutes from the bench does not count towards official statistics. Pennington, who had a background as a potter was one of 21 men available to Ian Millward against Hull and gave the pack a huge weight advantage. The outing was of course nothing more than a cameo by the comedian Johnny Vegas, real name Michael Pennington, who wore the number 30 shirt in the 28–18 win. Though time was short, there was a chance to run with the ball and even take part in a scrum.

BACK FROM THE WILDERNESS

Glyn Moses left the Newbridge Union club soon after the Second World War to join Salford. A superb full-back, he grew disenchanted with the club rather than his new sport so headed back to South Wales. Doing so meant he had effectively retired at the age of 23. There was no prospect of a return to his old club – although he attended games as a spectator – as his defection to professionalism made it impossible. Meanwhile Salford refused to let him play for the Cardiff club that had formed for the 1951/52 season or so much as an amateur side. Jim Sullivan was a huge fan of the player who knew he had much to offer the right team and the Saints coach landed him at Christmas 1952 after reaching an agreement over his registration. Sullivan was keen to land a dependable presence in the number one jersey after dispensing with Jimmy Stott and George Langfield

– both of whom preferred other positions. A debut came six days before a contract was signed and from that point until the season's end Moses picked up nothing but win bonuses after a run of 19 consecutive victories from the festive season on paved the way to a 6-point gap at the top as league leaders and a convincing win in the Championship Final. Moses only lost for the first time at Wembley Stadium where Huddersfield pulled off a tight win in the Challenge Cup final. Yet the Fartowners were heavily beaten a week later. A knee injury forced his retirement just before the decade ended.

THEY SAID IT ...

'Kevin Ward holds the British RL record for most stud marks imprinted on people's heads as a result of running straight over them. FACT!'

A Saints fan commenting on one of the attributes of the former prop forward.

FRANK CARLTON – FLYING FRANK

Very much an all-round sportsman, Frank Carlton excelled as an athlete among other sports. His pace set him apart from many runners and was coveted by Everton FC who placed him on professional terms. Thankfully Frank was considered not quite up to snuff as an Association footballer so was able to join St Helens where he enjoyed a long and fruitful career, winning trophies and international recognition before being transferred to Wigan. Introduced towards the end of the 1952/53 season he retained a place in the starting line-up for a number of seasons. A top try-scorer in three seasons, his biggest haul came in 1955/56 when he touched down 40 times. There were few better at wriggling past, busting through or simply evading backs. Just as certain a defender as he was an attacker, Frank developed a robust method of upending his opposing winger.

Despite that record and a crucial opening try in the 1956 Challenge Cup final five years into his spell, Frank's place in the side came under immense pressure and though one of his rivals, Jan Prinsloo, was transferred, Carlton also found himself surplus to requirements as Mick Sullivan was the preferred option on the left wing. Room had to be made and funds raised. 129 tries from 156 games proved to be a far better return than his successor and one of the best try-to-game ratios. Frank faced the Saints at Wembley in 1961 but was on the losing side.

THE CHALLENGE CUP

The trophy has been lifted by Saints a dozen times, all of which have been post-Second World War. Those victorious seasons are 1955/56, 1960/61, 1965/66, 1971/72, 1975/76, 1996, 1997, 2001, 2004, 2006, 2007 and 2008. A double with the championship has been claimed in 1965/66, 1996 and 2006. Strictly speaking, Saints were the last winners of the Challenge Cup, or at least the original trophy. After the 2001 triumph, the 104-year-old piece of silverware was retired as the metal around its neck was wearing considerably. That same year Saints won the trophy for the first and so far only time in change colours.

Along with Bradford Bulls, who completed the achievement first, Saints have lifted the trophy in England, Scotland and Wales. When Wembley went out of commission for redevelopment, the final was moved to other venues although St Helens are able to claim the distinction of winning the cup at the headquarters of each mainland Union federation – Murrayfield, the Millennium Stadium (formerly the Cardiff Arms Park) and Twickenham. The latter venue was used twice with Saints victorious on each occasion.

CHALLENGE CUP – ALWAYS A BRIDESMAID

The first of nine runners-up spots came in the competition's debut year and set a precedent of St Helens sides not always having the smoothest preparation. After making good progress through the five rounds sandwiched into a month towards the season's end, Batley would provide the opposition in the final at Headingley. There was little appetite for the venue at the Saints end and it was notable that the semi-final against Swinton had a larger attendance – almost 50 per cent higher. Many St Helens fans got to the match well after kick-off as their train to Leeds was late. Unfortunately, Batley were well on top when they arrived and remained so despite Traynor grabbing a try in the second half which reduced the arrears to 7–3. Billy Jacques missing the conversion meant the gap didn't reduce any further and another try for the Yorkshire side completed the scoring. Batley were paired with Saints in the opening round of the next season's competition, but managed to gain retribution for that defeat.

An arduous route was plotted to the next final some 18 years later as war raged across Europe. After being drawn away at each stage before the semi-final at a neutral venue and passing each test, Saints met a strong Huddersfield side in a showdown for the trophy. St Helens already had their work cut out but worse threatened to follow. The players were told their club's coffers were virtually bare and there would certainly be no bonus in addition to the ten shillings a game normally paid. The match at Oldham only attracted a joint lowest crowd of 8,000, though those paying customers could have come along to see nothing more than a game forfeited after mutiny erupted in the Saints dressing room. A strike was threatened over the lack of extra money. It may have been the case that the players believed their paymasters would relent at this late stage, but no compromise was on offer. Only the intervention of experienced skipper Tom Barton, one of nine local men selected for duty, who threatened to go out there alone, subdued the troops who simply couldn't compete against the Fartowners. A 21–0 half-time lead suggested there was nothing but pride at stake on the restart. Only a little was gained just before the close when Sam Daniels touched down in a 37–3 hammering.

St Helens made a debut beneath the Empire Stadium's twin towers in 1930 but again made life hard for themselves with more dressing room unrest caused by money. At the semi-final stage three men who had made the side one with every chance of carrying away all the prizes on offer – New Zealanders Trevor Hall, Roy Hardgrave and Lou Hutt – issued a list of demands to the club threatening to withdraw their labour if they were not met. Each had found jobs outside playing not to their liking and wanted £3 10s per week plus a huge £250 retainer to stay. It took a personal intervention by the town's mayor, Tom Boscow, to resolve what had quickly escalated into a very bitter dispute. Resolution came after the final was reached following a replay. £4 per week became payable with intermittent payments of £50 until the retainer demand had been met.

Non-footballing wages to the standard set out were also fulfilled. On top of this were performance bonuses equivalent to almost the average monthly salary of the typical spectator. Though top of the league ladder by a fair distance, the championship was lost and so too the cup. Underdogs Widnes finished in mid-table but were decent value for their triumph, especially as some Saints players seemed too intent on acting the goat ahead of the game. Varied acts of mischief including the setting off of stink bombs in the hotel conspired to disrupt preparation and crucial rest. There was also said to be an early morning return from a reception at the House of Commons with the town's MP – little wonder that some players looked sluggish in the 10–3 defeat. That could also be put down to the match day breakfast – a nearly inedible eggs and toast which proved a heavy rather than light meal. It was little reward for devoted fans like Alfred Townsend who walked to London in order to attend. All they had to cheer was Lou Houghton's early touchdown.

Heading to the capital took the game outside its northern hinterland for the first time and saw a virtual exodus from competing towns and cities. There was a massive migration for the 1953 final with Huddersfield providing the opposition. A highly physical edge was shown to the Yorkshiremen who managed to gain a lead with a controversial try from Peter Ramsden who many felt had been tackled before he bundled over the line. The stand-off had been on the sidelines for a number of minutes while the flow of blood from a nose injury was stemmed. Saints managed to level by the break and grabbed a lead by three-quarter time. Huddersfield regained the initiative but with eight minutes remaining it was level pegging once more until Ramsden secured a brace and, with it, the cup.

CHALLENGE CUP – FINALLY A BRIDE

Almost six decades on from reaching their first final and having been runners-up on four occasions, St Helens got their hands on the Challenge Cup in 1956 after beating Halifax. With the teams having finished second and third on the league ladder, an even match was expected. Seven days before squaring-up at Wembley the pair met in a Championship play-off at Thrum Hall with the hosts comfortable winners. But there were bigger costs. Having already lost Walter Delves from the second row, stand-off John 'Todder' Dickinson picked up an injury which kept him on the sidelines while Vinty Karalius's participation was very much in the balance until the day due to a large cut to his head. It meant Roy Robinson made his competition bow at Wembley becoming the first and to date only Saint to debut in a final. Though a tight affair until the break, Saints grabbed two converted tries with skipper and former Halifax man Alan Prescott crashing through just before time was up. 'Fax just had a penalty to show for their efforts in the 13–2 scoreline.

Wigan have been beaten by Saints in three finals. The first in the 1960/61 season took place with the mercury pushing towards three figures at pitch level. Despite going behind early in proceedings, St Helens went in 5–2 ahead at the interval during which players took on an energy drink consisting of lemonade, water and salt. The mix certainly should have refreshed them but Wigan dominated on the restart and thought they had gone ahead when former Saint Frank Carlton touched down, but they were punished for a forward pass in the move. A penalty then struck a post and Tom van Vollenhoven's try effectively sealed matters.

A RULE MADE TO BE BROKEN

The most controversial final came five years on. Rule changes have been a regular feature of Rugby League's continual evolution. Some have challenged gamesmanship – the most notorious arising from the 1966 final. Bill Sayer was brought to Knowsley Road just before Christmas 1965. He had been getting little football with the Cherry and Whites but slotted in to the Saints pack with aplomb and became one of the key figures in a ploy to thwart his old employers with his hooking skills. Offside was only punished by a kick for touch and then a scrum. Sayer was doing a sterling job in the mauls and as Colin Clarke, who had relegated Sayer to the Central Park club's 'A' team, was suspended for the final, Tom Woosey covered. The forward did his best but it quickly became clear there was a tactical advantage in gaining scrums, especially as without a tackle count the ball could be kept indefinitely.

Whenever St Helens saw a territorial advantage, an intentional offside infringement would take place. Often captain Alex Murphy would be the offender and Sayer ensured the game plan worked perfectly. Saints won a number of battles between the packs which was key in possession being dominated – so too the score with a convincing 21–2 victory. Killeen kicked 5 goals with 3 tries while Tommy Bishop, John Mantle and Murphy also crossed. As a direct result rule-makers decided that the same offence would in future be punishable by a kick to touch and then, vitally, a tapped restart for the wronged team. This ensured they retained possession as well as the advantage. 23 representatives attended and voted at the meeting, the motion somewhat ironically being carried by a 21–2 majority.

DAD'S ARMY VICTORIOUS

There are other intriguing tales from Challenge Cup finals. Wembley at full capacity in the glory of a sunny Saturday early in May took some beating, but with an ageing team nicknamed Dad's Army (due to half a dozen being in their fourth decade of life), Saints were underdogs in 1976. Kel Coslett and John Mantle were the eldest participants at 34. Widnes on the other hand were an up-and-coming side with some of the game's brightest young talents among their ranks. However, sometimes there is no substitute for experience and as the temperature gauge pushed 100 degrees the Chemics' young bucks charged at the St Helens line with such zeal that they quickly ran out of ideas then energy. Even so, the game remained finely balanced at 6–4 in Saints' favour. Widnes still expected to stretch away as the game wore on and the temperature continued to soar. They closed to within a point and Billy Benyon was taken off with a head injury which refused to stop bleeding. Peter Glynn came on and his fresh legs proved vital. A flurry of scoring saw Saints run out 20–5 winners.

BULLY FOR SAINTS

Three successive cup wins came against the Bradford Bulls with the first in 1996 ending a 20-year drought. Saints were in good form and overwhelming bookmakers' favourites. When Steve Prescott ran in two early tries it seemed that confidence was well founded, although the Bulls had turned things around by the break albeit only holding a 14–12 lead. As the final quarter approached, Bradford seemed set to extend a run of misery in the competition, leading 26–12 and looking comfortable. Or at least they did until Bobbie Goulding decided to examine a few flaws he had been busy identifying. The half-back decided there was susceptibility to the high ball and sent a trio of bombs close to the posts within a very short space of time. Each brought the desired effect and a mere five minutes separated tries from Keiron Cunningham, Simon Booth and Ian Pickavance. Nathan Graham at full-back couldn't cope and all 3 touchdowns were converted to put St Helens ahead once more. A try's width was a delicate margin, although it was extended when Danny Arnold went over. Robbie Paul ran in arguably the best try of the game to claim a hat-trick and narrowed the gap further with a conversion. Apollo Perelini settled things by beating attempts to stop him in front of the posts, completing the biggest comeback in Challenge Cup history. Reaching 40 points gave Saints the largest ever total in a final.

A year on, the pair reconvened. It was clear the Bulls had been working on improving their defence of the high ball but Saints employed the lower grubber kicks. Tommy Martyn touched a couple down and performed a full-length diving ankle tap on Danny Peacock when Bradford threatened to make a comeback. Karle Hammond's try just before the break also proved to be a decisive moment. Some earlier slack passing by the loose forward allowed the Yorkshire side to forge a lead but a show of body strength and sheer determination first held off five players then allowed Hammond to place the ball down. St Helens recorded their first ever successful defence of Challenge Cup.

It seemed especially appropriate that Super League's two power houses, St Helens and Bradford Bulls, should contest the 100th Challenge Cup final in 2001. Twickenham may have been an unusual venue but the unavailability of Wembley since the previous season meant the game could go on a grand tour. Both sides ensured that a marvellous advert for the sport was put on with some open rugby. Saints registered first and maintained a healthy lead which stood at 13–4 on the interval. Although the skies had been leaden above the players' heads throughout the opening 40 minutes rain had fallen sparingly. However, as the players re-emerged they were met with a torrential downpour. It was far from ideal for any side chasing the game but Bradford rarely looked troubled by the weather as much as they did by a resolute Saints side who only allowed them to reduce the deficit by a further 2 points. Although Saints threatened after soaking up the initial pressure, they spurned chances to extend the lead but did hem Bradford in via a superb kicking game from Sean Long. Only the video referee ruling a Tommy Martyn try out stopped St Helens adding to the lead. The Challenge Cup was added to the Super League and World Club titles. Three trophies in seven months was quite an achievement.

Huddersfield Giants, the Catalans Dragons and Hull have been beaten in the three most recent finals.

ERIC CHISNALL – BEING ERIC

There were always high hopes for Eric Chisnall's career, even an expectation as there was something not just different but special about the man who made a senior debut just after his 20th birthday. He had routinely looked a pace ahead of his contemporaries in the colts and carried on doing so at the highest grades. Like many who are quick of thought, he possessed lightning hand skills and the defences he could not ravage that way were beaten not only by his sheer size, but by lightning breaks. It often took more than one man to perform a tackle and if any of those in attendance left a gap, Eric would exploit it and offload to a team-mate. As the game moved from unlimited tackles to a maximum of four, it was a useful weapon in the armoury. There were also his own defensive contributions. Perhaps Chisnall's emergence corresponded with a period that St Helens were always going to dominate the sport, but there is little doubt that 'Chissy' played a massive part in the success everyone enjoyed, including his younger brother Dave.

On a personal level there were no high-profile man of the match accolades and, remarkably, he only got a handful of county and international caps. Comfortable in a number of roles across the forward line, Eric turned out in most of the second row positions as well as prop. All were demanding and just how he managed to keep so fit and injury-free given the hits he gave and took was remarkable – indeed, 53 appearances were made during the 1971/72 season as the club went deep into all competitions. It is a mark few others could match and never will with the season now much slimmer. Eric never missed even one final right until his time at Knowsley Road ended in 1982. He capped 16 seasons as a senior player with a spell at Leigh.

MARATHON TIES

A second round match with Morecambe went to a couple of replays after a 0–0 draw in the opening match of the tie was followed by the sharing of ten points at the coastal resort. The third and final meeting ended with a handsome home victory for St Helens. The pair met three times over six days and faced each other again in the league a week after their marathon 240-minute cup session. Knowsley Road played host once more and Saints recorded another win.

SAINTS AND SINNERS

The list of players to have turned out for St Helens and Wigan is extensive. The two clubs have not been shy of doing business with each other but in more recent years that tide receded. There is nothing to stop anyone moving after contracts have expired, but often at least another club has been sandwiched between these spells. There are still some notable tales.

Fred Roffey joined Saints in 1925 after a pay dispute could not be satisfactorily resolved. St Helens were keen to offer the type of deal their rivals could not fund plus the transfer fee and with good reason. The second rower had achieved and won much with Wigan. Though just past his 30th birthday, St Helens, a club which hoped to join the ranks of the heavy honours winners, thought he could do a similar job and help inspire those who had yet to attain such a level of success.

From the opposite perspective Eric Hesketh, who spent almost two years at Knowsley Road, was the son of long-serving Wigan chairman Thomas. Despite being a very adept, not to mention quick, stand-off and a well regarded amateur in the town, he bypassed the Central Park club joining Saints from Batley and only playing for the Riversiders twice. Each was in the War Emergency League rather than official matches with outings at points either end of the Second World War.

HE SENT IT

Proud Saint Alex Murphy decided to send a telegram – for those under 40 years of age, an SMS message via the medium of paper – to Central Park after St Helens won the 1966 Challenge Cup. It simply read: 'Roses are Red, Violets are Blue. St Helens 21, Wigan 2'.

DOWN AT HEEL

Don Vines was a versatile and sturdy forward who spent just less than a season at Knowsley Road. He also participated in another sport, or at least a sport of sorts. He was a professional wrestler who played the part of a heel – one of the bad guys who takes the boos and cat-calls from the audience he had incited by shouting in their direction and cheating before, of course, losing to the good guy. The size and strength of rugby players made a career in wresting quite appealing, though not necessarily as the heel.

Vines, who stood over 6ft tall, weighed more than 18 stones and was said to treat the crowd with nothing more than contempt was one of a number to earn quite a good living.

Knowsley Road has staged wresting bouts with the popular grappler Big Daddy fighting Mighty John Quinn of Canada in a specially constructed ring in front on the main stand. Contests between the two were popular. They sold out a 10,000 capacity Wembley Arena and attracted a very decent crowd on this occasion.

STEVE LLEWELLYN – ACCIDENTAL LEAGUER

Abertillery-born forward Stewart Llewellyn had an indifferent junior rugby career and only started playing again after his local side were unable to field a full team. An appeal went out from those who recognised him and, keen to do what he could, Llewellyn donned a pair of boots, scored a couple of tries and never looked back. That he came to Knowsley Road was also by pure chance. Saints were scouting a county game Llewellyn was playing in but with other targets in mind. The man who eventually became known to League fans as 'Steve' jumped at the opportunity when offered a deal soon after the game by the club's man in Wales, Albert Fairfax. He was swiftly followed by one of those who had been previously identified – George Parsons. Terry Cook, the three-quarter player who initially occupied attention, eventually joined Halifax.

The switch wasn't easy. In fact there was advice from a fellow countryman to go home and accept League wasn't for him. It possibly seemed the Saints management agreed as a week later he was dropped. But alongside natural talent – the Welshman was not only a speed merchant but a quick thinker and good ball handler – determination saw him through. So much so that he was top try-scorer in just his second season and maintained that status for a number of campaigns. Only injuries stopped that record increasing. Confidence was also key and once that came in spades, he put in some very creative performances, laying on a number of scoring opportunities for others with both his hands and feet. Llewellyn wouldn't have looked out of place as a centre but only performed in that role a few times. The supposed twilight of his career was the most productive in terms of honours – with a championship and the club's first Challenge Cup success. Llewellyn was a scorer on each occasion he made it to Wembley.

His St Helens career ended in 1958. There may have been a few more years had it not been for a certain Tom van Vollenhoven knocking on the door. The South African's claims were becoming irresistible and Llewellyn retired. That van Vollenhoven and only one other flanker, Les Jones, have ever bettered Llewellyn's touchdown record since perhaps underlines the contribution he made.

THE UMPIRE STRIKES BACK

Mark Elia was a decent cricketer although he played in an unusual venue for the game during 1990, taking part in matches across the USA. The New Zealander also umpired a game in North America when Australia met Pakistan in a one-day encounter. A versatile centre during his playing days, Elia coached skills in Australia but now stands as an umpire on a fairly permanent basis. He is a member of the Cootamundra and District Cricket Umpires' Association in New South Wales.

STAR OF RING, FIELD AND SCREEN

Adam Fogerty embarked on a career as a heavyweight boxer before turning to rugby. He had the physique for both and with 18 wins from 19 fights, mostly by way of knock-out, it seemed he could travel some way in the ring. However, the level of opponents he fought both in the UK and Australia were often open to question and he called it a day after 85 rounds as a professional. Signed from Halifax Blue Sox, Fogerty made just 63 appearances including 9 as a substitute over 4 seasons including 15 in the first Super League campaign before seeing out his rugby career at the Warrington Wolves. Along with stage roles plus turns in soap operas and other television shows, Adam Heywood Fogerty – as he is often billed – has featured in a range of films including *Up 'n' Under* where his rugby skills came in handy.

GEORGE PARSONS – PREACHING TO THE CONVERTED

One of many Welsh Union stars tempted north in the late 1940s and certainly one of the most sought-after in the immediate post-war period, George Parsons came to Knowsley Road and fitted well into the second row.

Born on the same day as Queen Elizabeth II, Parsons was seemingly set for stardom in his teens, turning out for Cardiff, Newport and then Wales. He had already played in unofficial Victory Internationals and at 19 years of age became the youngest forward to wear one of the coveted scarlet jerseys. A 6–9 defeat at the Arms Park against England wasn't a result to remember but the occasion certainly was – especially as it proved to be his first and only outing. Less than a year later, after some machinations with the governing body and approaches by almost two dozen League clubs, he joined Saints who had sent him a couple of letters expressing their interest. He freely admitted the only St Helens he knew was the rugby and cricket ground in Swansea.

Still shy of his 22nd birthday when changing codes, he was an immense man standing more than 6ft tall and weighing 15 stone. He was extremely mobile due to an insistence by his early mentors that he play as a centre to improve his handling. Never a consistent try-scorer he did at least offer a contribution every year but only managed to make double figures in the 1952/53 season. That tally included a hat-trick in the Championship semi-final with Huddersfield. His all-round game came to the fore when George took over kicking duties for a couple of seasons. An offer to play but also coach Rochdale Hornets, a club he debuted against for St Helens, saw him leave but there were winners medals from every competition – Lancashire Cup, Championship, Lancashire League and Challenge Cup. Welsh and Great Britain caps were earned as well as a taste of leadership. Parsons was selected to captain the side during an end of season tour of the valleys he spent his formative years in. Bursting with pride Parsons played on his old ground at Abertillery. He had a brief spell with Salford before finally hanging up his boots. He remained in St Helens after retiring, becoming a manager at Pilkingtons, a magistrate and a town councillor for the Liberal Party.

KNOWSLEY ROAD – OLD TRAFFORD AND WEMBLEY ROLLED INTO ONE

Super League authorities may consider Knowsley Road an antiquated ground and a possible threat to St Helens's franchise, but it has been likened to Old Trafford and Wembley Stadium. Or at least 1960s versions of those venues for a film. It must also be added that the set designers also provided something of a make-down.

A biopic of George Best's life and footballing career – entitled *Best* – included footage shot just off Dunriding Lane during the late 1990s. The Eccleston Kop was a makeshift Stretford End – with a little camera trickery it was made to look almost as imposing as the terrace where Manchester United fans gathered in such huge numbers. Either MANCHESTER UNITED or UNITED was painted at various points of the ground needed for other outside shots. A replica of the commemorative clock to mark the Munich Air Disaster was attached to the Main Stand. The TV gantry was used in recreating elements of the 1968 European Cup final with the Directors' Box transformed into Wembley's Royal Box for the presentation of the trophy.

IT'S WIDE TO WEST

Confident of sealing a win that would see them through to the 2000 Grand Final eliminator, Bradford Bulls fans counted down the seconds of their qualification play-off. Quite simply it appeared nothing could go wrong, especially when the ball went dead, but St Helens gained a penalty and after quickly getting the ball back into play, they took it short. Trailing 11–10 Saints were still pegged back close to their own line. Defences had been on top throughout the game and seemingly hemmed in. With the time keeper's hand virtually hovering over the hooter, there seemed no chance of gaining so much as a point to force extra-time. The ball was moved little more than a dozen yards on the left when, more in desperation than hope, Sean Long kicked across the field. There was no realistic route down the pitch. Long's lob was fielded by Kevin Iro who exchanged passes with Steve Hall. With his route blocked, Sean Hoppe was introduced. Boxed in, the Kiwi flipped the ball back over his shoulder for Hall. Tim Jonkers had little more than a second with the ball before finding Long who after a burst left found three-quarter Dwayne West.

Time was now up and although inexperienced, the 20-year-old who started as a replacement showed fantastic temperament. Failing to be rushed he took a look around him and close to touch on the left beat a couple of defenders before an offload to Chris Joynt. Bradford could still take no risks and commit a foul as a kicked penalty would edge them out. Besides there was still 40 metres left and seemingly enough cover. Once the move ended for whatever reason the game would be over. However, Joynt evaded a tackle and despite Anthony Sullivan sprinting on the inside screaming for a pass his skipper went for the line, stunning the Bulls with a game-winning touchdown. The ball had been passed nine times from each side of the field and back and virtually its full length.

JOHN MANTLE – PRINCE OF WALES

Losing giant forward John Mantle was a huge blow to Welsh Rugby Union. He was an outstanding sportsman as a schoolboy and at university where he played the fifteen-man code, soccer and athletics. He had not made too many outings for Newport before breaking into the national side acting as a full-back and then on the right wing. In club games he operated as a back row number eight where his athleticism and physical muscularity served well in the line-outs. It served St Helens well too. When the offer came to go north Mantle readily accepted, slotting in well and taking the new surroundings in his more than ample stride as he saw out the 1964/65 season when Saints carried off the Lancashire League and minor Premiership.

Those prizes only sound like small beer as the rest of his Knowsley Road career was little short of glittering. Each trophy was won and often more than once, the most coveted arguably being Championships and Challenge Cup four and three times respectively. Welsh and Great Britain caps were a given. Fitness was key to John's longevity which saw him represent St Helens in virtually every forward role as well as a centre. Early on he also turned out as a flanker. Mantle left St Helens at the grand old age of 34 after 11½ seasons, moving on to serve other clubs. He was still playing, albeit it in the lower divisions, until the ripe old age of 40.

SOCCER AT KNOWSLEY ROAD

Knowsley Road has played host to soccer with Liverpool Football Club's reserves utilising the facilities on a relatively ad hoc basis for three seasons between 1998 and 2001. Super League running during the summer made the arrangement work well, although the Reds often decided to take games elsewhere once Saints began their campaigns.

The ground has also provided the largest stadium for clubs below the top tier of the non-league scene. Playing at the ninth level of the game's pyramid means St Helens Town, who have shared the ground since 2002, may not have worried about the 17,500 capacity being breached. But the North West Counties Premier Division side report that figure as the point at which the house full signs will be put up. The New St Helens Stadium will increase that capacity by 500.

LANCASHIRE CUP

Saints enjoyed a purple patch through the 1960s winning the competition seven times and reaching the final on a couple more occasions. Taking in the seasons just before the decade began there are a couple more runners-up spots and between 1958/59 and 1964/65 a record, shared with Wigan, seven consecutive finals were reached. Swinton were faced in four of those five years with three consecutive finals pitting Saints against the Greater Manchester outfit. Remarkably, following a heavy defeat of Oldham in 1968, St Helens failed to reach a final for the next 17 years.

Throughout the war years the Lancashire Cup was suspended although its Yorkshire equivalent continued with Saints taking part from the 1942/43 season onwards, but always falling at the first hurdle when aggregate scores over two games were tallied. In two of the three campaigns Wigan provided the opposition.

LANCASHIRE LEAGUE

Over much of its history the Rugby League Championship had an overall winner plus two county champions representing Yorkshire and Lancashire. In the very early years matches would only take place within a club's own county. When a league ladder encompassing all clubs from the same county playing each other home and away plus a sole game against teams from across the Pennines was instituted for the 1907/08 season, results from all games were totted up to decide the national picture with the intra-county games counting towards those parochial leagues.

Saints won nine titles and were runners up half a dozen times before the structure was disbanded in 1970. Three successive crowns were lifted in the mid- to late 1960s. The full list of winning seasons are: 1929/30, 1931/32, 1952/53, 1958/59, 1959/60, 1964/65, 1965/66, 1966/67 and 1968/69.

For a couple of seasons in the early 1960s the county championship was replaced by the Eastern and Western Divisions in which a group of five teams played in a round-robin style tournament and the top four then played-off. A final would be held on a neutral ground. Saints finished top of the Western Division and after beating Oldham in the semi-final met second placed Swinton at Wigan. A 10–7 triumph won the trophy.

JAMIE LYON – NETTING AN EEL

Jamie Lyon had a controversial early career Down Under but was loved at Knowsley Road. Despite staying just two seasons – like another Aussie centre who only had a short stay with the club, Mal Meninga – he is rightly judged as one of the greats. It seemed an unlikely transfer when struck in August 2004 as aged just 22, Lyon had announced his retirement. This came just a couple of days after his Parramatta Eels side lost the opening game of the Aussie season. He had two years of a lucrative contract remaining with many suggesting his roots in the countryside being a factor in his apparent unhappiness. If he couldn't take the Sydney suburbs many wondered how he would take to St Helens when a deal was announced. Gold Coast Dolphins, Penrith Panthers and Canberra Raiders had made bids after a move back to Lyon's junior club, Wee Waa Panthers, was brokered. It took AUS$150,000 to buy out the player's contract with Parramatta and AUS$300,000-a-season salary. It was money well spent as his debut in February 2005 suggested.

The plaudits just kept coming. A goal-kicking centre he scored 22 tries and created just as many for Darren Albert and Ade Gardner on his outside. When 42 goals were added, Lyon amassed 172 points and was named Man of Steel at the end of his first campaign. There was similar recognition from his peers. Lyon would also shine kicking in open play. He did so to great effect when covering at stand-off in a game against Warrington and creating three tries. Despite his efforts the club's trophy cabinet was empty. Quite a lot changed 12 months later. Only a relief kicker in that first campaign he took over the responsibility from Paul Sculthorpe in his second season and largely as a result was the Super League's top scorer as Saints claimed a Grand Final and Challenge Cup double. Lyon made no secret of his determination to go back home and though it seemed Parramatta would lure him back to the NRL, Manly Sea Eagles were successful in their bid with a four-year contract. There remains a hope among Saints fans that he may return at some stage. Such aspirations were given a boost late in 2008 when, after an approach by Warrington was revealed, Lyon suggested that he would like to return to England and St Helens before his career finishes. If that wish can be realised it will offer a chance to add more points to the 610 garnered from just over 60 games.

A SPECIAL AND REGAL TROPHY

For over a quarter of a century clubs battled it out for a trophy carrying the name of a cigarette manufacturer. Mostly contested over the early months of a campaign, it generated revenue at the gates, broadcasting and a decent prize fund from the sponsors. The competition had many guises – it was used to promote a host of brands and had four incarnations as a result. The sport's secondary knock-out competition is one St Helens have a poor record in. Just two final appearances in 25 years have yielded a single triumph and it remained the one trophy Saints had yet to win or so much as reach a final in prior to January 1988.

When Leeds held a 14–9 half-time lead, that run seemed destined to continue. It couldn't have been fully realised at the time but just seconds before the hooter Neil Holding put in what proved to be a vital drop goal as the second half saw an early try and conversion remain unanswered, although Garry Schofield struck an upright with a late kick at the posts.

That narrow win is the only success. The Super League era created a new emphasis within the game and a fresh calendar meaning this tournament was abandoned after Saints lost the last final staged to Wigan. With the exception of a few football venues, club grounds hosted the final with Knowsley Road selected as a neutral venue for successive seasons between 1977 and 1979.

A LOT OF GOOD WORK FOR CHARITY

As Premiership, not to mention championship, runners-up to double-winning Wigan, Saints made their sole Rugby League Charity Shield appearance prior to the 1992/93 season and lifted the trophy quite comfortably in Gateshead courtesy of a 17–0 win.

JACK ARKWRIGHT – START OF A DYNASTY

Though not the club's leading points scorer or appearance maker, Jack Arkwright was a genuine great of the game and a star for St Helens immediately before the Second

World War and only wrested from Knowsley Road when Warrington offered a club record £800 fee. An England international while with St Helens at Wilderspool, he added to the sole cap earned then, won Great Britain honours and toured the antipodes. Remarkably he was sent off twice in the same game against Australia. His marching orders came after hitting a player but the opposing captain requested that the referee rescind the decision. The official complied but there seemed more than good sportsmanship on the agenda. Revenge was the key to this compassion and it was not too long before Arkwright raised a fist to the man who had pleaded his case.

Prior to his departure Arkwright racked up an impressive 159 points from 174 games. Excellent value from an amateur signed for £50. A second-row forward as he developed, Jack began as a prop. His biggest low as a Saint was missing the 1930 Challenge Cup final against Widnes. The decision was perhaps expected as he had seldom played in an extensive run up. Heartbroken by all accounts, he was not even allowed to ride in the team coach so travelled to Wembley on a motorbike to cheer his team-mates on. He was also devastated at the loss they suffered at the Chemics' hands. New to the side, Arkwright may have expected another chance at a Wembley outing. It never came although he was a key member of the side to win the Championship Final two years on. The odd game at loose forward highlighted his versatility but his point-scoring was priceless as an occasional goal-kicker not to mention decent try-scorer from his berth, his best contribution being 22 by the 1932/33 season's close.

THERE'S ONLY ONE STAN BEVAN

Or maybe not. Although there is no official word to corroborate this tale, the story goes that as part of a spending spree St Helens were hoping to land a promising forward called Stan Bevan but wound up plucking another player of the same name from near obscurity in Wales. There was little option but to field him on arrival and although he managed 11 games over the final two-thirds of the 1910/11 season, it seemed clear there was something missing from Bevan's skill set. He left the club virtually without trace although there is a suggestion he may have joined St Helens Recs.

LANCE TODD TROPHY

The award made to the player determined by the Rugby League Writers' Association to be the man of the match in a Challenge Cup final, the Lance Todd Trophy, has been won on 12 occasions by St Helens players. There are a few distinctions. Leon Pryce and Paul Wellens are the only joint winners while Sean Long is the sole player to grab a hat-trick of awards – none of which were at Wembley. Just 8 players have earned the distinction despite being on the losing side. George Nicholls is the only St Helens player to do so in 1978 after a narrow 14–12 defeat to Leeds. Although awarded at Wembley (and other prestigious venues when the Twin Towers were decommissioned), it was handed over at a dinner hosted in Salford's ground The Willows. Now other venues are used.

1956	Alan Prescott
1961	Dick Huddart
1966	Len Killeen
1972	Kel Coslett
1976	Geoff Pimblett
1978	George Nicholls
1997	Tommy Martyn
2001	Sean Long
2004	Sean Long
2006	Sean Long
2007	Leon Pryce and Paul Wellens
2008	Paul Wellens

HARRY SUNDERLAND TROPHY

A trophy named after an administrator in both Australia and Britain, awarded to the star man in Championship or Premiership deciders and now Grand Finals. It has been won by just seven St Helens players.

1966	Albert Halsall
1970	Frank Myler
1976	George Nicholls
1977	Geoff Pimblett
1985	Harry Pinner
1993	Chris Joynt
2000	Chris Joynt
2006	Paul Wellens

ALAN PRESCOTT MEDAL

Only one Saints player has an honour in his name. The Alan Prescott Medal is given to the man of the Test series against Australia played in England. The award is minted in silver and is named in recognition of the outstanding contribution made in these matches since Prescott's Test debut in 1952, followed by additional series as skipper. In particular perhaps, it recognises the match at Brisbane in 1958, known as 'Prescott's Match' or 'The Battle of Brisbane', after the captain played all but four minutes with a broken arm.

MAN OF BRONZE
– KEIRON CUNNINGHAM

Part of the club's new stadium design includes a bronze statue of the player who won most votes when a choice was put to supporters. In a poll Keiron Cunningham secured 10,138 votes compared to the 8,820 Tom van Vollenhoven received. Paul Wellens trailed in third with 1,501 while Alex Murphy was a little further back on 1,284. The next couple of shortlisted candidates were in three figures – Alf Ellaby on 249 just ahead of Vince Karalius with 203. Positioned on Chalon Way since its unveiling in March 2010, it will move when the stadium is complete.

OTHER MEN OF THE MATCH

Awards have proliferated for the stand-out performers in finals. The now defunct Lancashire Cup began making an award in 1974. Mal Meninga was the sole St Helens winner a decade later. Similarly, Paul Loughlin is the only man to lift the accolade in the Regal Trophy following a decisive role in a narrow win.

MEN OF STEEL

Possibly the most sought-after award available to Rugby League players, the Man of Steel, has rarely owed its gift to trophies or individual success. Although won by a Saints player in just its second year, the honour was a long time returning to Knowsley Road. However, once it did at the start of the new millennium St Helens men began to dominate with only three of the next ten awards having gone elsewhere. With so many good players the reasons are understandable.

1978 George Nicholls	2005 Jamie Lyon
2000 Sean Long	2006 Paul Wellens
2001 Paul Sculthorpe	2007 James Roby
2002 Paul Sculthorpe	2008 James Graham

THE PLAYERS' PLAYER

The Players' Association has an award for its best player of each season and has been won by five Saints players.

1999   Sean Long
2000   Paul Sculthorpe
2005   Jamie Lyon
2006   Paul Wellens
2008   James Graham

Graham is the only Saint to be crowned Young Player of the Year earning that honour two years before receiving the senior award.

CLIFF WATSON – A CAPITAL GAIN

One of very few Londoners to turn out for St Helens, Cliff Watson played Rugby League and Union in his youth. It was perhaps a secret he could keep while turning out in the West Midlands as a forward before answering a newspaper advert Saints placed directly appealing for anyone looking to switch codes. Watson was keen to be reacquainted with the professional game and attended a trial, ceasing to be an amateur at the turn of the 1960s. However, Watson made a debut knowing he had only six games to prove his worth. Utilised as a prop forward he passed all examinations with flying colours, claiming a Challenge Cup winner's medal after an outstanding all-round performance and try-saving interventions; incredible that he should take to the game's biggest occasion and stage so well with less than a dozen games under his belt. After spending almost 11 years at Knowsley Road, Cliff took up the challenge to prove his worth in the demanding Australian competition for a few seasons following an invitation from ex-Saints colleague Tommy Bishop who had been named as Cronulla Sutherland player/coach. He subsequently served Illawarra club Wollongong Souths.

That debut season with St Helens was the start of a wonderful era for the club, but so too for Watson who, for the most part, was only ever left out of a side when injury intervened. Aside from the silverware there were 30 Great Britain caps with a large clutch of those as skipper – although he was the only player to be sent from the field twice in Tests against the Aussies. A member of the renowned 'pack of aces' which won all the domestic prizes on offer at least once, Cliff was so strong that opponents would double if not treble up on tackles – and still not floor him. More than a mere battering ram and muscle man, the front rower also made subtle ways through defences and is also said to have had one of the best hand-offs in the business.

COACH OF THE YEAR

Just three St Helens coaches have been named coach of the year. Daniel Anderson is the only man to claim the honour twice.

1996   Shaun McRae
2001   Ian Millward
2006   Daniel Anderson
2007   Daniel Anderson

BERNARD DWYER – SAINT BERNARD

As those who watched St Helens and Bradford Bulls in the 1980s and '90s would testify, Bernard Dwyer was never viewed a star unless he played for your team. Capable of playing in most forward roles, he acted as a hooker and loose in the pack over the course of much of his debut campaigns while being introduced to the team gradually. Only five seasons into his senior career could Dwyer consider himself a regular. His hunger for work on the field simply never seemed sated and strength-sapping performances from the first minute to the last failed to weaken that resolve. Some statistics place his tackle count at more than thirty over 80 minutes. Yet the locally produced Dwyer wasn't just about intensity and those hard yards. A keen observer of the pattern of play he would often ghost into moves having been completely undetected until crashing over the line. Sheer strength would see him through when his runs were tracked. Goal-kicking duties were assumed while Paul Loughlin struggled with injury during the 1991/92 season and contributed more than 100 points to his career total.

A losing finalist at so many of his initial attempts to gain silverware, Dwyer missed out on those competitions which were won through hard luck with injuries. That was until the 1993 Premiership Final – his only honour as a Saints player. Bernard joined Sonny Nickle and Loughlin plus quite a bit of cash as makeweights in the deal which brought Paul Newlove to the club in November 1995. His last few campaigns were blighted with injuries but at just 28, he had years ahead of him and proved an astute signing for Bradford with whom he won the Super League title and that highly coveted Challenge Cup. His four previous attempts with Saints and then against his hometown club with the Bulls had ended in defeat. He may well have achieved a little bit more in the game but bicep injuries forced him to call it a day not long after Bradford won another Challenge Cup with Dwyer one of the interchange options on the bench.

TOP TRY-SCORERS

Tom van Vollenhoven	392
Les Jones	285
Alf Ellaby	280
Stewart Llewellyn	238
Roy Mathias	217
Anthony Sullivan	213
Alan Hunte	189
Doug Greenall	188
Frank Wilson	176
Keiron Cunningham	175
Alex Murphy	175
Paul Wellens	175

ROY MATHIAS – WING WIZARD

One of the speediest flankers in Rugby Union, and subsequently League, Llanelli's Roy Mathias had initial worries about switching codes – especially when so young and with just a couple of seasons under his belt. A chance to turn professional came not too long after he debuted for Wales. Fast, strong and with a very distinct style of running, Mathias was a nightmare to stop. The most robust of tacklers would usually be undone by a jink inside or even to the very edge of the whitewash. Pure agility would also see him dive through to cross the line. Little wonder, then, that he became the club's top-scorer in most of the seasons he spent at Knowsley Road. The 1973/74 term was his best with 40 tries claimed – the best since Tom van Vollenhoven's heyday.

Powered by his tries and the benefit of some extremely gifted centres, Saints landed virtually every prize on offer. Able to work on either wing, Roy would sometimes swap during games but as his legs started to lose their electric jolt he took a place in the pack over his last season and a half with the club – mostly in the second row or as loose forward. The tries dried up but he still made it past a double century in a Saints jersey and remained a regular up until the time he left. He even had the odd spell back on the wing and, all told, made over 400 outings.

LET THERE BE LIGHT

Knowsley Road's floodlights were installed in the mid-1960s and officially switched on by Sir Harry Pilkington prior to a challenge match against the Other Nationalities on 27 January 1965. It cost £10,923 to erect iodine lights in five groups of ten on either side of the pitch.

FLOODLIT'S FINEST

A wider installation of floodlighting across grounds saw the introduction of specially commissioned televised competitions, the BBC2 Floodlit Trophy being the most noted. The brainchild of wildlife documentary maker David Attenborough, who was then head of the channel, it ran between 1965 and 1980. The chance of silverware and the additional money raised even saw those grounds not able to host night-time games move towards installation of lighting systems. All matches were played in the evening – or at least should have been. Due to the oil crisis of the early 1970s, the 1973/74 final was played during the afternoon as floodlight use was severely prohibited at the time. Novel rule changes were introduced such as a limit on the number of tackles before a scrum was held to four. This was later increased to six.

Saints were the most successful team in the competition's history making 7 appearances in the final – although losing 5 – including the inaugural run which was also played at Knowsley Road. Castleford who were unbeaten in their 4 finals won a close encounter courtesy of 2 penalties. Further tight losses to Leeds and Wigan made the team even more determined to succeed at the fourth attempt against Rochdale Hornets.

Individual scoring records in finals are shared quite liberally among a number of players and inevitably a number of Saints are prominent. Ray Mathias and Peter Glynn have scored a couple of tries and share the record with two more players. Similarly Kel Coslett shares the record for most goals in finals. As a result of those successful kicks he also shares the record for the highest number of points recorded, with Glynn and others. No player managed to feature in all 7 finals although Billy Benyon and John Mantle played a part in the first 5. Les Jones was too young to participate in the first 2 but did grab a nap hand of appearances between 1970 and 1978.

FUSED WIRES

It seems Warrington are a club struck down by a Knowsley Road hoodoo. Their winless run at the venue, which includes just 2 draws, goes back beyond the Super League era to 1994 and stretches to 22 games. Home or away the Wolves have had no success against the Saints from 2001, despite some winning positions being held in the closing seconds.

The opening season of summer rugby set the recent trend as Warrington were edged out at Wilderspool despite leading 24–17 with 7 minutes to go. A moment of madness by Lee Penny, who was sent off for a blatant high shot on Alan Hunte, allowed Bobbie Goulding to narrow the gap. His kick from wide was by no means easy but brought Saints within a converted try of victory. A break by Derek McVey 3 minutes from the close allowed Ian Pickavance to touch down after accepting a fine pass then spinning away beneath the posts. Goulding was never going to pass up the easy chance presented. Remarkably Warrington could have snatched victory back but Chris Rudd's penalty in stoppage time (albeit from long range) had neither the power nor direction needed to slide between the posts.

The most stunning return from a seemingly impossible position came in 2005. The hosts led 16–4 at the Halliwell Jones Stadium with 10 minutes remaining only to be hit by a 6-minute blitz and edged out 18–16. Tries from Darren Albert and Mickey Higham pulled the difference to just 2 points. Nerves were jangling on both sides but Keiron Cunningham found the winning touchdown with the last action of the game after Jamie Lyon hoisted the ball hoping someone would be able to profit. Just 3 seconds remained when the Aussie kicked. Albert got a hand in, doing just enough to pat it on for Cunningham who lurched over the line. However, it took the video referee some time to signal that all was fine with the players' positions. Warrington attempts to take the ball and Cunningham's own handling was examined before the big screen flashed up 'try'.

When the pair met again later in the season Sean Long landed a penalty – in the process he pulled equal with Austin Rhodes at 1,921 career points. Another late show seemed to have snatched a tie from the jaws of defeat but Warrington couldn't cover all the options during the next set of six and with just seconds remaining, Long produced a 40-yard drop goal to edge Rhodes into fourth on the all-time lists but more importantly claim 2 league points. The match was one which was high on entertainment with the lead regularly changing hands. A last-minute Jason Hooper try and conversion from Wire old-boy Paul Sculthorpe brought another 2-point away victory in 2004.

NEVER KNOWING
WHEN THEY ARE BEATEN

On the subject of comebacks, two of the most stunning came in finals separated by 25 years. The 1971 Championship Final was nearing its end with Saints trailing Wigan 10–6. It would have been worse and the deficit insurmountable had Colin Tyrer not missed four attempts at goal. However, those errors didn't look like proving fatal when John Mantle was dismissed for retaliating against an overly physical attempt to stop him 15 minutes from time. Bill Ashurst scored a drop goal to increase the lead and, a man down, there seemed no way back. Even when Bob Blackwood squeezed through to the corner after a move which swept from one side of the pitch to the other, and Kel Coslett held his nerve to improve the score from near the touchline, there was still a point separating the sides with little more than a minute left. It meant Saints had to take a chance. The simplest method would be a drop goal which Johnny Walsh tried to land from an incredible distance and a tricky angle. The tension, length and charging defence seemed to get on top of the centre who pulled the effort wide, but without enough power to reach the posts it remained in play and bounced to Billy Benyon who despite a shoulder problem, crossed the line. There was little time for Wigan to respond and most of the precious few seconds that remained were taken up by Coslett's conversion which made it 16–12. Wigan claimed that Benyon was blatantly offside but the officials disagreed. Wiganers dubbed him the one-armed bandit due to the injury he was carrying and their contention that the trophy had been wrongly whipped from beneath their noses. Saints, who had finished second to their great rivals, were champions.

PLAYING YOUR SUBS

Although Rugby League is now very much a 17-man game with substitutes having specific roles within the game plan and twelve interchanges allowed, four players have to start on the bench. The modern era has seen two players reach more than a century of games through introductions during the play alone. Maurie Fa'asavalu leads the way with 157. James Roby is the only other centurion having reached that mark during the 2009 Super League season and has added to that tally since. His ability to destroy tired defences from dummy half with not just speed but an intelligence which still belies his youth, made this sort of deployment a handy tactic for a succession of coaches. Although Keiron Cunningham's retirement will see him start more games, the Whiston-born Great Britain international is likely to exceed the Harlequins RU-bound Fa'asavalu's number before too long.

CLUB CHAMPIONSHIP

This tournament was something of a one-season wonder which saw all teams compete in a merit league, with points awarded for various factors and a system so complicated involving league placings and records in knock-out cups that it is better left in the *Life on Mars* era of 1973/74. The Championship tournament between the top 16 had been scrapped courtesy of two divisions being created, something was needed to take its place. After home wins over Workington Town and Castleford and then a semi-final victory at Leeds, Saints met Warrington in the final. Central Park played host and Saints lost out 13–12. Alex Murphy missed 6 drop goal attempts and Warrington thwarted some very precise attacks even if they were low in number. Kel Coslett who had placed 3 kicks between the posts looked to find the late equalising point with the game's last action but from 40 yards his drop-kick attempt drifted inches wide of the uprights.

TOP TEN GOAL-SCORERS

Kel Coslett	1,639
Sean Long	989
George Lewis	850
Paul Loughlin	842
Austin Rhodes	815
Geoff Pimblett	608
Bobbie Goulding	548
Len Killeen	408
Paul Sculthorpe	392
Stanley Powell	320

SUPER LEAGUE SUPER SAINTS

St Helens were crowned champions of the first Super League season simply by holding Wigan Warriors in second place courtesy of a single point once each and every top-flight side had played the other home and away. This had been the method of deciding the order since 1974 but after two seasons of the league leaders receiving the accolade, a Grand Final play-off was brought in to decide the title holders. Until 2007 and the start of a run of 3 successive defeats to Leeds Rhinos, Saints had a faultless record with 4 appearances and 4 wins in the Old Trafford showpiece.

1999	v Bradford Bulls	won 8–6
2000	v Wigan Warriors	won 29–16
2002	v Bradford Bulls	won 19–18
2006	v Hull FC	won 26–4
2007	v Leeds Rhinos	lost 33–6
2008	v Leeds Rhinos	lost 24–16
2009	v Leeds Rhinos	lost 18–10
2010	v Wigan Warriors	lost 22-10

Prior to all but one of these three meetings with Leeds, Saints had finished as league leaders but only received a silver salver for being top of the pile after 27 tough rounds of rugby. In 2005 St Helens became the only side so far to end the regular season top but not make the Grand Final after a narrow defeat in the eliminator.

EUROPEAN CHAMPIONS

The advent of Super League allowed the winners to be crowned European rather than mere domestic champions, the inclusion of Paris St Germain in the inaugural season providing that opportunity. However, St Helens claimed that honour 26 years earlier courtesy of beating 1970 Le Championnat de France de Rugby à XIII holders RC Saint-Gaudens over two legs. A 30–11 win in Southern France at Stade Jules Ribet just before Christmas was followed by a far more comprehensive 62–0 home victory after the season closed. The 6-month hiatus due to the usually packed fixture list possibly explains why the challenge was never played again.

MAL MENINGA – SHORT BUT SWEET

The pre-eminence of Australian rugby during the early 1980s made many clubs think about bringing in some of their number. Then, over the summer months of 1984, came the announcement that Mal Meninga, who had helped his nation batter Great Britain's best players, would be joining St Helens for the coming campaign. It would come at a cost – an immense £30,000. It would also involve the additional procurement of Brisbane Souths team-mate Phil Veivers but every penny proved not just worth it, but well spent. Winning the Lancashire Cup was a tangible result and victory over Wigan in the final was one in which Mal played a full part. A stunning early try set a marker for the standard which would follow. Drawing players towards him ten yards inside his own half, Meninga created a huge gap but decided not to offload. He had previously allowed others to profit from the space he created, but this time decided to rely on his strength as he bustled past Mark Cannon and Shaun Edwards, handing-off the former then contemptuously swatting the teenage full-back away. Meninga was an unrelenting force of nature over 80 minutes. It seemed he was all over the pitch and had a hand in everything.

It was little different in the Premiership Final when a tight game had seen Saints grab a couple of leads only to be pegged back courtesy of George Fairburn's efforts. However, despite Hull KR continuing to threaten the line, they were denied a chance to pull level when Mal intercepted a David Hall pass then sped 40 yards to the line with half an hour gone. Fairburn had decent pace on him and tried to barge the Aussie into touch. Flying in with every ounce of his energy and weight, he made contact but Meninga barely stuttered let alone looked like going to ground and charged through. Another lapse by Hall, who was looking to mount an offensive but threw possession away, allowed Mal to take the ball almost the entire length of the field as he turned on the burners to leave Fairburn – who this time thought better of a launch – and Gary Clark in his wake. The giant centre made that sort of finish a trademark. For good measure he also kicked 8 goals by the close of his debut season.

Although injuries meant he never returned to Knowsley Road as a home player and by consequence made just 31 appearances for the club, there was little doubt of the esteem Meninga was held in – especially by Saints fans. Indeed, Australia's tour match in November 1986 was held up for 10 minutes while a pre-match presentation was made to him. Almost 14,000 acclaimed someone who was a brief servant but undoubtedly a great player.

TOP DROP GOALS

Just 10 players have reached double figures when trying to gain those sometimes all-important extra points in a game.

Harry Pinner	73
Neil Holding	44
Geoff Pimblett	28
Tommy Martyn	25
Sean Long	23
Augustine O'Donnell	20
Roy Haggerty	20
Bobbie Goulding	13
Paul Bishop	11
Paul Sculthorpe	10

NOT SUCH A SWEET STAY

Mark Bourneville was a New Zealand tourist brought to the club on a short-term basis towards the end of the 1989/90 season. Nicknamed 'Horse' due to his distinctive high-kneed style of running, he made 5 appearances including 3 from the bench before drifting away and actually becoming a French international. That figure includes a debut against Warrington which was halted within 4 minutes. A strong gust of wind took a corrugated roof sheet off the Main Stand which almost struck Des Drummond before impaling itself in the turf. With such huge dangers to players and fans, the match was abandoned. Bourneville was on the bench for the restaged match.

THEY SAID IT ...

'Before I came over, I had a bit of a flat spell and I came to England to pick up my confidence. Today I have gained some valuable experience and done my confidence a power of good. Let's hope I can continue to play well and win a few more games for St Helens.'

Mal Meninga after an awesome display in the 1984/85 Lancashire Cup final.

MATCH ABANDONED

In 1944 the War Emergency League Boxing Day clash with Wigan was abandoned after Saints fans invaded the pitch to remonstrate with the match referee. Just 23 minutes had been played with Wigan leading 12–3 and Saints fans felt the officials had helped create that deficit.

IF THE CAP FITS

Tommy Barton and Frank Lee became the first St Helens men to gain national recognition when selected to face a team consisting of Other Nationalities on New Year's Day 1906. Barton was not the first choice at full-back and was only called up after a late withdrawal. Although he had played more regularly in three-quarter roles, recent performances in the position at club level – he made 5 appearances in just under a fortnight due to the busy Christmas period when 4 games were crammed into just 7 days – impressed the selectors.

LIONS CAPTAINS

Eight players have skippered Great Britain in either Tests, World Cup and Tri-Nations series games while with Saints.

Alan Prescott	17
Frank Myler	9
George Nicholls	5
Harry Pinner	4
Alex Murphy	3
Tommy Bishop	2
Les Fairclough	1
Paul Sculthorpe	1

PAUL SCULTHORPE – SCUL AND BONES

Scully was not only the domestic game's most expensive player but the world's costliest forward at £370,000 when signed from Warrington in 1997. Chris Morley went the other way to help smooth the wheels a little more. The man who would eventually skipper the club through a prodigious spell of silverware collection gave a service which justified that outlay. Many players are able to operate within the backs as well as the forwards, and do so at the drop of a hat depending on the team's needs, but perhaps not with the same effectiveness or creativity as Sculthorpe. Few forwards who concentrate on their power – which Sculthorpe also possessed in bundles – are able to step up and pick out those vital balls which rip otherwise solid defences to shreds. On top of that came an ability to kick goals from all manner of angles and distances. Those duties were bestowed on the Lancastrian at the same time he was asked to cover more extensively at stand-off due to the absence of Sean Long and Tommy Martyn respectively.

A scorer of more than 1,000 points and having achieved the feat of landing 300-plus goals and a century of tries, there is no danger of statistics not telling the whole story of Sculthorpe's contribution. When Chris Joynt left the club, the man who made vital contributions to so many important games including Grand Final and Challenge Cup victories was the natural choice as leader. He also captained Great Britain not to mention England and was also fully deserving when crowned Man of Steel by his peers for back-to-back seasons in 2001 and 2002. There may well have been another award had it not been for a disappointing run of injuries suffered over his final few campaigns. Scully would not have wanted to miss any game but particularly galling, despite the result, was being forced off within the opening minute of the 2008 Challenge Cup final with a dislocated shoulder suffered when putting a crunching tackle in on Hull's Todd Byrne. This proved the final straw and a culmination of setbacks which led to something of an early retirement in 2008 after a well-deserved testimonial season.

YOUR NUMBER ISN'T UP LIPPY!

Graham Liptrot may have been a skilled and consistent hooker, but he sometimes made the odd lapse. Taking Les Boyd to ground with a fair if robust challenge during a game with Warrington was something the Wire's tough-as-teak forward would accept as incidental rough and tumble, though it probably meant equally harsh treatment when the Aussie got his chance to dish out the same medicine. However, Liptrot coming in as the third man to hold him then put his forearm into Boyd's face was a huge issue. Boyd had a deserved reputation in his homeland landing two lengthy bans before getting a fresh start in England.

Saints' players and particularly Harry Pinner could barely believe what they had witnessed and more so that Lippy seemed totally unruffled about the possibility of retribution, the hooker's reason being that his number had been held up on the touchline moments before the challenge. Unfortunately he hadn't realised that the board would be flipped over when the replacement was actually made. Consequently a trot to the safety of the sidelines turned into a walk of dread – back towards play and the inevitability of vengeance being exacted. That came in the next scrum. Liptrot asked for someone to take over his duties but found no volunteers. He left the field on a stretcher soon after the ball emerged.

TOP TEN POINT-SCORERS

Kel Coslett	3,413
Sean Long	2,625
Paul Loughlin	2,004
Austin Rhodes	1,921
George Lewis	1,835
Geoff Pimblett	1,388
Paul Sculthorpe	1,246
Bobbie Goulding	1,209
Tom van Vollenhoven	1,176
Len Killeen	1,161

THREE TIMES A CHARM

It is far from unusual for players to enjoy two spells at a club. To date, 44 Saints have had at least a couple of spells at Knowsley Road but only one has enjoyed 3 separate stints on the books. The hugely popular not to mention powerful Sonny Nickle joined from Sheffield Eagles in 1991, landing trophies plus Test caps before leaving as part of the world record deal which brought Paul Newlove to Knowsley Road 4 years later. After a period of similar length with the Bradford Bulls ended, there was delight at his recapture and three more trophy-laden seasons followed before he joined Barrow Border Raiders. Sonny failed to make an appearance for the Cumbrian club before arriving back. Barrow would have liked nothing more than to allow Nickle a run in the Northern Ford Premiership but were not allowed that pleasure due to a 9-game suspension picked up in the final game of that second St Helens spell. Four of those games had already been served but there was no opportunity to serve the remainder before Ian Millward brought him back early in the 2002 season. It may only have been for a season but it was to the delight of both fans and player, even if he did miss out on the two big finals of that third period before seeing out his career at Leigh Centurions.

AN UNSUNG HERO

Kevin Ward was 33 when he joined St Helens but was far from a player seeing out his career. The Yorkshireman had been brought in to augment a youthful team but also wreak the same type of havoc he had made St Helens suffer throughout most of his lengthy career with Castleford. There was more to Ward than his awesome power. A centre before becoming a prop he had good pace and few could match his handling. A Challenge Cup winner with Cas and Premiership winner in Australia with Manly, he added a Lancashire Cup medal and may have had longer to win more at Knowsley Road save for a broken leg which not only proved difficult to recover from but was in danger of being amputated. The injury suffered in a full-blooded clash with Wigan meant he watched the 1993 Premiership win from the sidelines. Ward is one of just eight Englishmen to win a NRL Grand Final.

GEORGE NICHOLLS – BEST FOOT FORWARD

When asked to pen a best ever 13, fans of both Widnes and St Helens would have to include George Nicholls. A silky smooth ball-player who glided past opponents and created a huge number of tries, he touched a few down in his time too. This man was a forward rather than a half-back and at the time he tormented defences, many of his contemporaries were strictly ball-up-the-jumper battering rams only concerned with making yards and giving others a chance to cross the line. He could do that and was a massive presence in defence too. It took £9,000 to prise him away from the Chemics, his hometown club, not long after he helped Great Britain lift the World Cup after beating the Australians. It was a hefty sum for a player quite close to a third decade but few ever felt it wasn't money well spent. A loose forward at Naughton Park it was a position he only covered in at Knowsley Road playing mostly in the second row. He also deputised at prop on a handful of occasions.

Over 200 games for Widnes with 38 tries and a goal in the credit column was some return for a dozen and a half seasons. Nicholls was also part of a team pushing for honours which did not quite mature until after he left, but with St Helens he was a winner of a league championship, Challenge Cup and a couple of Premierships. He is also one of just three men to claim the Harry Sunderland and Lance Todd Trophies plus be named Man of Steel at a season's end. His time with the Saints ended with an outing from the bench against Widnes a week past his 36th birthday. At that point, time was catching up with George; unable to make the same type of bursts, he was largely held in reserve until a match was entering its later stages and some guile was required. Still the creative force, he failed to score a point in any of the matches which brought his overall tally just shy of a double century. Top-flight rugby may now have been a stretch, but in the lower rungs he enjoyed a season-long swansong at Cardiff City.

MINNIE WAS NO MOUSE

An imposing Welsh prop forward in both Union and League, Carmarthenshire-born John Warlow could look after himself and dished out his fair share of blows. However, during the 1966 Challenge Cup semi-final with Dewsbury he found a seemingly unlikely champion. His landlady Minnie Cotton, widow of George, a Saints wingman during the 1920s, ran on the pitch to remonstrate with one or two of the Yorkshire side's forwards who she felt had dished out some overly rough treatment to her lodger. Dick Lowe was singled out and hit repeatedly with an umbrella which he threw into the stands while Trevor Walker, who had also been involved in the Warlow incident, restrained the assailant.

For his trouble Walker was given a piece of Minnie's mind and a few digs of his own – with the brolly and then more after it had been discarded. It took a few policemen and some more strapping players to persuade Minnie that she should desist. In a Championship final with Halifax a few weeks later the redoubtable Mrs Cotton set about a few more targets of her ire. This time a handbag was the weapon of choice. Frank Barrow and John Mantle made up an unlikely tag team which decked four 'Fax men.

Minnie Cotton had red and white running through her veins. Her grandfather Thomas Topping was a member of the club's committee, she would travel to the ground with the team and her mum was a laundrywoman who washed kit along with other items at their home on Kirkland Street. It was perhaps inevitable she would meet a husband at Knowsley Road, be that a player or a fellow fan.

UNBEATEN RUNS

Saints' winning run of 25 games encompassed the concluding 13 games of the 1985/86 season and the opening dozen of the next term. This constitutes both the longest perfect run and unbeaten sequence since two divisions were instituted in 1973. Sixteen consecutive matches were won on the road during the 1952/53 season creating a league record which still stands. The team went unbeaten away from Knowsley Road over the entire season as the fixtures they did not win on their travels were tied.

WORLD CLUB CHAMPIONS

Europe's champions meet their Australasian equivalents each year to decide which can be labelled World Champions. The game dates back to the mid-1970s when Saints took on and lost to Aussie equivalents Eastern Suburbs. However, that game was unofficial and there was an 11-year hiatus before the next clash. Then the meeting only took place on an ad hoc basis until 2000. That same year marked St Helens' return with a whacking defeat to Melbourne Storm. Saints edged out the Brisbane Broncos 12 months later recording the first of 2 wins.

The record in this event is:

1976	v Eastern Suburbs	lost 25–2
2000	v Melbourne Storm	lost 44–6
2001	v Brisbane Broncos	won 20–18
2003	v Sydney Roosters	lost 38–0
2007	v Brisbane Broncos	won 18–14

A wider pool of clubs – in fact all 12 Super League outfits and each of their 10 Australian/New Zealand counterparts – battled out for the title of World Club Champions and the not too small matter of prize money totalling AU\$1,000,000 (or £640,000). Six rounds of games were played – in both hemispheres – with Saints scrapping into the quarter-finals courtesy of a play-off with Paris St Germain. Cumbersome, expensive and with losses estimated in the region of £3 million, there was little further appetite for this style of contest, especially as no British club did better than reaching the last 8. The format was rested for a few seasons before being brought back as the one-off between the 2 competitions' champions.

KEL COSLETT – KING KEL

The nickname 'King Kel' was not a nicety based on alliteration – it was a more than accurate description for those watching from the sidelines. There is barely an accolade – team or personal – this son of Carmarthenshire poached from the Union code in 1962 failed to secure. All his club records – most appearances, most points, most goals scored – are unlikely to be bettered, although they would have increased even further had conversion and penalty duties not been transferred to Len Killeen for a few seasons during the mid-1960s. It was only over this period that Coslett failed to kick more than a century of goals in a season as he was utilised on a relief basis. There were also injuries at that time which caused an absence from the 1966 Challenge Cup and Championship finals. The points came rolling in from his kicking opening game and just kept flowing. They increased once responsibility had transferred back from Killeen to Coslett. There was barely an area of the field Kel didn't feel confident of successfully landing the ball from. Tries were by their very nature less forthcoming than those goals, but built steadily and increased when a change of position was required.

Initially a full-back, he switched to loose forward partly due to the emergence of Frank Barrow, but also courtesy of a leg break in 1965. This also cost him that highly prized goal-kicking role although Kel excelled in that position, controlling the tempo and direction of play. Fleet of foot, Kel was also a true genius at the dual disciplines of pushing teams on and holding things together when under pressure. Named club captain after standing in for Cliff Watson during the early part of 1971, Coslett was able to take his game into a new dimension. Kicking not just for points but touch and possession was becoming a more important facet of the game. Very often leads would be built and retained on the basis of this art. Saints had one of the foremost practitioners. There were also spells back in the number one jersey along with odd matches in the role of centre or as a member of the pack.

Trophies were thrust into the Welshman's hands on something of a regular basis, even if there were two barren seasons until the championship was won by some distance in 1975. A final season brought Challenge Cup and Premiership success and drew a veil over 13 campaigns with the Saints. After coaching Rochdale Hornets and then Wigan, Kel had a spell in charge at Knowsley Road between 1980 and 1982, but starved of funds to supplement an inexperienced if sometimes promising nucleus of a squad, he left the job but has racked up more than 30 years' service in other roles since.

COME IN NUMBER NINE

Although Keiron Cunningham is not the only ever-present over 16 Super League seasons, he is the only player to have served the same team throughout that run and to have retained the same shirt number – 9.

NEIL HOLDING

Local lad Neil Holding got his chance to stake a first-team claim when Saints were very much a team in transition. Many of the players that had formed the bedrock of successful sides had moved on or simply hung up their boots. While there was a small core of experience, the emphasis was very much on youth and the scrum-half debuted in this period just 8 weeks ahead of his 17th birthday. Although he did well when called upon, it was not until the start of the next campaign that he could call himself a regular, albeit in a number 6 or number 7 shirt. Often he would be an ace up the sleeve introduction from the bench. He was a hugely talented and creative footballer who used all manner of kicks plus clever runs, shimmies and dummies to buy space for himself or others.

An old head on a very young pair of shoulders, he was not only the largest contributor to others' points tallies, he also ended two seasons as the top-scorer overall, kicking conversions and penalties plus drop goals and touching down more than his fair share. Through some bleak years he had a huge say in matters as St Helens began to pick up trophies again in the mid-1980s and then as they went close over the seasons which followed. Unfortunately the last 3 of his 13 campaigns in a red V saw him play a slightly more limited role before he extended his career with Rochdale Hornets and Oldham. There was a brief return before retirement but only as cover so no chance of adding to the 343 appearances, 145 tries, 84 goals and 44 drop goals combining to total 739 points. It was sad Holding could not join the elite band of players to strike a century of tries and goals for the Saints, although often those single-point efforts were vital in either the score or changing the pattern of a tight game.

PAUL LOUGHLIN – POINT MACHINE

With ball in hand or at his feet Paul Loughlin was a hugely devastating force and turned in many match-winning performances, even as a teenager. A debut from the substitutes' bench and a few more stints as a replacement were the fledgling steps taken by a player who could and would interchange between full-back and a central role. It was the latter discipline which saw him gain his lengthiest run in the side and create chances for the increasingly prolific Barrie Ledger with some trademark shuffles past opponents and pace to burn. Although there could be a reliance on sheer power, Loughlin would also make use of the blind side more effectively than anyone else when there seemed no way through massed ranks. In just his second season he racked up a record tally of points from a single game, grabbing 40 against Carlisle in a 112–0 rout. The Cumbrian side may have been minnows but such prolific point-scoring and inspired work made international honours inevitable.

By the time a new decade began 1,000 points had been reached and Loughlin was firmly on his way towards a second millennium but the team's fortunes waxed then waned. Consistent rather than irregular challenges for honours – to which he was a central figure – were undone by the departure of other key players who either returned to their homeland or joined other clubs. However, like a metronome the Sintelliner continued to provide a throbbing pulse and leadership. The man on which success over the early Super League era was built, Bobbie Goulding, took over the goal-kicking duties and stunted the copious amount of points so far amassed, although the 2,000-mark was reached. Had it not been for an overriding desire to bring Paul Newlove to St Helens in 1995, with Loughlin among others used as bait to increase the value to £500,000, then there is a possibility that he could have troubled Kel Coslett's goal and points aggregate records. With Bradford there was more than a hurrah to Loughlin's career even if his stay lasted just two years. He not only won but was instrumental in their claiming of the Super League title in 1997 although they lost successive Challenge Cup finals to St Helens which meant he had lost 5 times at Wembley.

TEENAGE KICKS

On 6 March 1937 – the eve of his 16th birthday – Harry Briscoe made his Saints debut as a scrum-half against Swinton. It was the first time he had ever worn a Saints jersey having not been given an 'A' team game or even a trial. His only experience had come at schoolboy level where he had certainly impressed, but many thought he was more of a soccer player than rugby footballer. Unfortunately not long into the Second World War he was killed in military service at just 19 years of age.

PAYING A HEAVY PRICE

After being found guilty of misconduct by placing bets on St Helens to lose, Sean Long and Martin Gleeson received suspensions of 3 and 4 months respectively. It took some hours for a disciplinary committee to hand down that punishment along with large fines of £7,500. The pair were said to have used their knowledge of a weak team selection by Ian Millward over a busy and demanding Easter programme just weeks ahead of the 2004 Challenge Cup final. Injuries were the reasons given for so many absentees with certificates produced to prove each player's plight. Long was one of those left out, so received a lesser punishment even though there was no evidence or even a suggestion that Gleeson did anything other than his level best against Bradford Bulls.

Normally a close game would be expected, hence decent odds were available for that result would have been viewed inevitable with inside information on the team to be fielded – a Saints defeat. With prior knowledge, bookmakers would have offered much shorter odds. The wagers earned the pair, who claimed they knew nothing of regulations preventing their actions, £900 each. Long was able to make a return before the season ended, playing in the last round of the normal season against Bradford, but Gleeson missed the remainder of the season and left the club during his ban joining Warrington Wolves for £200,000.

HAT-TRICKS

When friendly games are included, the number of Saints hat-trick performances totals 591.

TOP OF ELEPHANT LANE

Thatto Heath has produced a number of great players, with St Helens being the main, if not only, beneficiaries. However, it would not appear to be a landmark on the Rugby League map everyone recognises. That possibly came as news to one of its many noted sons, Roy Haggarty, who seemed a little surprised an Australian TV reporter could not quite put his finger on its whereabouts. So when questioned further about the precise location the second row forward helpfully added, 'Top of Elephant Lane.'

DUGGIE GREENALL – LIKE A BARREL

Duggie Greenall was a slight lad who many would never have believed capable of making it in a hard-hitting game like Rugby League. However, he enjoyed more than 13 years in the Saints first team and an encounter with the centre – he changed to that role after outings as a stand-off and winger – could be a bruising one for an opponent. Duggie was accused of wearing a plaster cast on his often-bandaged arms by some he beat, but there was no truth in the claims. That 12-stone frame was also good for slipping past the line and wriggling through to create opportunities for others, including the highly prolific Tom van Vollenhoven.

Greenall was rooted to the club. He literally lived next door to the ground and had more than a couple of relatives in the Saints' employ, both playing and non-playing staff. Later on, one of his grandsons joined the ranks.

A debutant in the game's first post-war season he worked hard, though other than international Tests, gained little reward. Saints often threatened but lifted none of the most prestigious silverware for two decades. Trophy-winning seasons in the mid- to late 1950s had Duggie in tandem with Steve Llewellyn then van Vollenhoven. The latter may have been the greatest wingman ever to wear a red V but his development and many say his understanding of the game after switching codes arrived via Greenall. Just days before the new decade began, a decision to allow the loyal servant a chance to leave was granted with a move to Wigan.

NUMBERS GAME

In the era of squad numbers Neil Rigby has worn the highest – 36. He was one of 9 debutants when earning his spurs as a replacement in a game at Catalans Dragons in August 2006. Daniel Anderson fielded a weakened side just ahead of the Challenge Cup final. With a long trip and temperatures in Southern France often pushing 100 degrees, there was no prospect of risks being taken although accusations of the game being virtually thrown were dismissed by both the performance and result. Despite trailing 20–6, and being a team with an average age just above the late teens, St Helens scored 16 unanswered points and would have won but for a piece of Stacey Jones trickery in the last minute.

SIGNS OF THE TIMES

Like many clubs Saints have sported the town's crest on their jerseys but perhaps the most fondly remembered badge is the stickman saint complete with halo. It was very similar to one used in *The Saint*, a popular TV series of the 1960s starring Roger Moore, then Ian Ogilvy when the show was brought back a decade later (Moore had since found world-wide fame by playing James Bond). The character Simon Templar's initials ST being an abbreviation for the word saint led to the name, and he was essentially a do-gooding mystery-solving adventurer.

This design stayed until the 1990s when a crest returned. Later in the same decade this was in turn replaced by a specially designed entwined S and H which stayed until the formation of a St Helens Sporting Club encompassing the town's soccer team in 2001. When the relationship soured, a return was made to that knotted S and H.

A HELPING HAND IN NORTH AMERICA

Although the USA may consider Grid Iron to be their national sport, Rugby League is growing swiftly across North America – quicker than any other sport. Saints have done their bit to help and in 2010 a partnership was established with the Canadian Rugby League. Mementoes made their way across the Atlantic with equipment aiding the Canada team prepare for their debut in the 'War of the Shore' tournament in Sea Isle City, New Jersey, during late July. A. Cooper, a player from the 1930s, is the only known Canadian to have played for the Saints.

There is another link. Former 'A' team man Ron Stott was loaned out to Liverpool City a few years before emigrating to Canada and helping form a Union team in his new home. In order to honour his hometown club, the Sarnia Saints were born.

A WING AND A PRAYER

Christopher Maude Chavasse had a brief spell at Knowsley Road but is one of the more fascinating characters to have worn a rugby jersey, let alone a St Helens one. The eldest son of the Bishop of Liverpool, on account of arriving 20 minutes before his twin brother Noel, he was a promising athlete and alongside his sibling contested the 400 metres at the 1908 Summer Olympics. Unfortunately, though well-placed in their individual heats, because semi-final places were only available to winners of the 16 races staged, each brother failed to progress. A chaplain in the services during the First World War, Christopher was made an officer of the Order of the British Empire's Military Division and received four other decorations, most for gallantry. An ecumenical life beckoned during peace-time though his appointment as the Bishop of Rochester came six months into the next world war. He also served as the first Master at St Peter's

College – founded by his father – which eventually became part of the University of Oxford.

His religious life began in St Helens as an ordinary parish priest and reverend with a unique way of gathering crowds. A church band would play and one of his colleagues would shout 'stop thief' after Chavasse started running. His athletic prowess meant he could not be caught by those seeking to apprehend him and a throng quickly gathered. Once he decided there were sufficient people following they were led back to the band which had played on and began a sermon. Outside his time as a preacher, Christopher played League after his spell in Union with Liverpool. Religious duties meant he mostly turned out for the 'A' team although he did manage half a dozen outings with the first XIII.

An exceptionally fast winger he caused a stir in January 1911 when after selection for a league game with Wakefield Trinity he was sent off the field some 30 minutes in. The referee was forced into that action as Saints already had their full complement. Jimmy Prescott was plying his trade down the flank after Chavasse had failed to report at the club's pre-match headquarters. After penning his weekend sermon into the small hours and giving it some more thought the next afternoon, he fell asleep in front of a warm fire. Late and worried about letting his team-mates down, the 'flying curate' enthusiastically bounded on to the pitch in order to atone. The impromptu but well-meaning pitch invasion saw him reported for an act of ungentlemanly conduct.

Whatever grade he played at, the club captain would often rebuke swearers to ensure no offence was caused to 'the parson' as Chavasse was also known.

OLYMPIC IDEALS

St Helens have fielded a number of players to have participated at the Olympics Games. South African winger Attie van Heerden, who found great fame at Wigan well before a brief stint with the Saints late in his career, was also a 400 metre hurdler at the 1920 games in Antwerp. British sprinter and 100 metre record-holder Berwyn Jones, a convert from the Welsh Union scene, was viewed as a potential competitor for Tokyo 1964 after helping Great Britain win a bronze medal in the 1962 European Championship 4 x 110 yards relay, but took the chance to try out in League which ended his chance to run or play the other code as both sports were strictly amateur. He served Wakefield Trinity then Bradford Northern and won international recognition before becoming a Saint. However, his career in Lancashire was short-lived amounting to just 4 games ahead of a premature retirement at just 29 years of age.

One man who had Olympic ideals far from his mind was local man Albert or Ned Bacon. The self-proclaimed fastest man in the county – although he had some evidence – could earn very decent money as a prize racer and via waging on his performance. Both were something he did until almost 40 years of age. Who could blame him when a sprint race lasted 10 seconds compared to the 80 minutes he needed on a rugby field to earn so much less? That said, over a few seasons he spread out 16 first-team games plus many 'A' team matches and as a wingman took heavy knocks that just never happened on a running track.

TOMMY MARTYN – TOMMY GOD

St Helens have boasted a range of great stand-offs of which Tommy Martyn is ultimately one in a very long line, but in tandem with Bobbie Goulding and then Sean Long he formed a couple of devastating half-back partnerships that helped Saints dominate the Super League era. In fairness, even on his own the man signed from Oldham would have been a match-winner in either attack or defence, something he often proved and on the biggest stage of all when helping win the 1997 Challenge Cup final. A couple of tries, two very different set-ups for Chris Joynt and then Anthony Sullivan, he put his side well on top and an ankle-tap tackle earned him the Lance Todd Trophy. Big performances in big matches, no matter if silverware was up for grabs or not, were a hallmark of his game.

Tommy's kicking game and tactical acumen were a match for any number 7 he played alongside. He also added goal-scoring to his often vital eye for a touchdown. Signed at a point when Knowsley Road was building towards the near future by picking up the cream of young talent, the 22-year-old finished his debut campaign as top scorer having turned out in three different positions. It all marked him out as a good prospect and his handling made him a superb option at centre. A leader by example, on the field he was a natural choice as captain and consistently lifted silverware. He also became just the second player to register a century of tries and goals for St Helens. Injuries were a bugbear with routine knocks added to broken arms and reconstructive surgery on each knee. However these only slightly limited his appearances as he generally – 1995/96 season excepted when he missed an entire campaign – played through, undergoing much-needed repairs and surgery during the off-season. He left the club midway through the 2003 season to join hometown club Leigh as a player/coach. It was a natural progression for a visionary player and drew a decade of service to an end. From just over 200 appearances he garnered 743 career points, 127 tries, 105 goals and 25 drop goals along with every medal on offer.

SEAN LONG – THE LONG AND THE SHORT OF IT

One of many Wigan-born players to serve the Saints and become a Knowsley Road hero, Sean Long was released by the Warriors having failed to show too much of the flair which would eventually make the scrum-half one the most crucial players in the country's best side of the early 2000s as a Widnes Viking. But there was enough to convince Ian Millward this was a man who could replace Bobbie Goulding and the Australian's judgment was quickly validated. Point-scoring was one measure of his ability and breaking Super League records for the tally collected in just his third season was another. That mark, 284, was shattered a year later with 20 tries and 136 goals amassing 352 points. Cup matches boosted the tally to 420. From either side of the pitch and seemingly any distance or angle, goal-kicking was key to a mechanical and prolific accumulation of points.

A first thousand then a second millennium were reached in just over 7 years. Had it not been for a couple of lengthy injury absences plus suspension caused by a decision to bet on his side suffering a heavy defeat in 2004, it is inevitable that 3,000 points would have been attained before he left to join Hull FC in 2009. He would also have reached the century of tries and goals becoming just the third player to achieve that feat. He fell just 13 touchdowns shy and lies in second place on the all-time list of point-scorers behind Kel Coslett. Another gauge of Long's worth and influence on the team is the silverware collected – often courtesy of big performances in key games – including 3 Lance Todd Trophy wins in 6 years. Saints and the Brisbane Broncos were separated by just 2 points in the 2001 World Club Challenge when Long found 11 of the 20 needed to beat the NRL champions. Victory in the 2002 Grand Final was snatched by the landing of a tense conversion just before time.

SUPER LEAGUE HIGHS

Over the course of the 15 Super League seasons to have been played, counting the regular season alone, the individual and team records are below. Goals figures include drop goals.

Most appearances
| 348 | Keiron Cunningham | 1996–2010 |
Most career tries
| 146 | Paul Wellens | 1998– |
Most career goals
| 846 | Sean Long | 1997–2009 |
Most career points
| 2,041 | Sean Long | 1997–2009 |
Most tries in a season
| 28 | Paul Newlove | 1996 |
Most goals in a season
| 125 | Jamie Lyon | 2006 |
Most points in a season
| 352 | Sean Long | 2000 |

Most tries in a game
5   Anthony Sullivan   v London Broncos (18/9/1998)
5   Kevin Iro   v Huddersfield Giants (1/5/2000)
Most goals in a game
12 Jamie Lyon   v Castleford Tigers (14/8/2006)
Most points in a game
32 Jamie Lyon   v Castleford Tigers (14/8/2006)
Most points scored by the team
78 v Leigh Centurions (4/9/2005)
Biggest losing margin
70 v Leeds, lost 70–0 (23/7/2004)

DOUBLE REGISTRATION

For 2010 Super League players under 23 on 31 August in the year preceding a season commencing were eligible for dual registration if they were outside the top 20 best paid professionals within a squad. Essentially, they would be loaned out to a Championship or Championship One club although subject to recall to the parent club. Saints shared prop forward Jake Emmitt with Leigh Centurions. Dual-registered players can only turn out in one fixture per scheduled round. Emmitt's form with both clubs saw him brought back for a number of top-flight and cup games.

St Helens share many reciprocal arrangements and relationships with Leigh at various levels designed to ensure each club mutually assists the other. Aside from the Centurions, Saints share understandings with Widnes Vikings who have taken a number of players on loan and with whom they will ground share during 2011 until the new stadium is ready.

THEY SAID IT ...

'St Helens have really got their tails between their teeth.'
**Commentator Malcolm Lord mixing his metaphors when
providing considered opinion on a game.**

SAINTS IN DREAMLAND

Since the Super League era commenced, a panel of journalists
and broadcasters cast votes to select a dream team made up
from all elite clubs according to position. St Helens players
have been prolific members of these XIIIs although they did
miss out totally in 2003 for the first and only time. Keiron
Cunningham has made seven appearances making the cut
at dummy half in 1996, 2000, 2001, 2002, 2005, 2006 and
2008. The highest number of players selected at the end of a
season is five achieved in 2005, 2006 and 2008.

THE TALL GUY

Australian forward Wayne McDonald, who signed a 2-year
deal when leaving Hull Sharks but spent just a season with
St Helens, is the tallest man to grace Super League at 6ft 7in.

POINTLESS ENCOUNTERS

It is rare that a game remains without score for more than the first quarter, but 0–0 draws were once quite common after time had been played. The Northern Union's inaugural season saw St Helens fight out the ultimate stalemate with Wigan, Oldham, Wakefield Trinity and Brighouse Rovers. The first three were in initial meetings with each of those opponents. Such results eventually became fewer and a meeting with Broughton Rovers in January 1931 was the last in a league game. A third round tie with Bradford Northern at home in March 1950 was the last in a Challenge Cup match. The replay was lost 11–0.

Excluding those who played the Saints only once, just three teams have failed to register a single point against the men from Knowsley Road. Birkenhead Rangers were frustrated over the course of five meetings including the first encounter in November 1901 which was abandoned. Altrincham failed in their two cracks and conceded 46. South Shields had just 29 unreplied points put past them over a couple of meetings in the 1903/04 season.

St Helens were unable to gain a reply to the 38 points Sydney City Roosters scored in the 2003 World Club Challenge and must wait until both sides win their respective championships to redress the situation.

NEVER BEATEN

Just 5 teams are unbeaten against St Helens in official matches. Melbourne Storm are one and there are 2 more Aussie outfits who have a 100 per cent record against the club – Cronulla Sharks and Penrith Panthers who have each played Saints twice. Closer to home, Manningham finished champions in the opening Northern Union league season with Saints just one of the teams who failed to beat the Yorkshire outfit over the course of a couple of matches. A split along county leagues due to the sheer number of new members brought into the competition ensured the two sides wouldn't meet again as Manningham switched to purely Association football as Bradford City in 1903, well before the two leagues combined once more.

The most unlikely team to have such a proud record against one of the game's giants is Acton and Willesden. The Londoners enlisted for the 1935/36 season hoping to establish themselves as one of two permanent League sides in the capital. Operating costs proved their downfall and even decent crowds failed to provide enough money to sign top-quality players. They folded but among their 13 wins were a couple against St Helens; a 5–2 victory at Knowsley Road early in the season was followed by a 5–0 home win at Park Royal.

SUNDAY TRADING

Sunday games only became the norm for most clubs in the late 1970s and professional teams had been banned from competing on a Sunday until 1967. Even the traditional fixtures on Christmas and Boxing Day were moved along the schedule when falling on the seventh day of the week.

St Helens did not choose to embrace the change for some years and only moved to Sunday afternoon games on a regular basis at the beginning of the 1977/78 season. A friendly with Pilkington Recs was played on the Sabbath with the first top-grade match being against Swinton in the Lancashire Cup a fortnight later on 21 August 1977.

BARRIE LEDGER – SAINT LEDGER

An unlikely looking winger he may have been, but Barrie Ledger was highly effective in the role and had a turn of pace, not to mention turn of foot, which beguiled those trying to stop him reaching the try line. He was to all intents and purposes a carbon copy of his father Eric, though their careers were separated by the best part of three decades. His weaving and ability to sell the dummy was second to none – even when there seemed nowhere to go he would evade capture and reach the line. Playing outside Paul Loughlin for a sustained spell had a positive effect too. Carefully nurtured through the youth system he made an impressive if not devastating start to his senior career with both the ball in his hand and with the boot. Quite often he would nudge the ball beyond the full-back, knowing his feet would more often than not take him clear of any cover and in for the 3 points. He also proved a steady kicker at the posts. However, although certainly good enough to be a designated man to convert tries and penalties, he was generally employed as relief when others such as Clive Griffiths and Sean Day were unavailable.

His skills and tactical acumen also made him a good option as a half-back should the need arise. Barrie spent a couple of games at stand-off. Unfortunately due to his playing during a transitional period at Knowsley Road – the great side of the 1970s had been well and truly broken up – there were fewer medals than Barrie deserved and except for the 1985 and 1988 Premiership Finals – the latter being his last game as a Saint and a defeat by a strong Widnes side – he failed to get in on the scoring action in the few finals he did appear in. Perhaps a little unceremoniously he was shipped out to Leigh while still seemingly having so much to offer. Just over 200 appearances with the first team yielded a little under 600 points in official games. Had he remained, there is no doubt he would have reached a century of goals as well as tries. He may well have at least doubled each tally.

LAST HURRAHS

Probing from dummy-half has been a hallmark of Keiron Cunningham's career and as the end of his playing days and St Helens' tenure at Knowsley Road beckoned, the pair combined to provide compelling finales.

In the last game of the regular league season, Castleford, trailing by 4 points having just seen their advantage turned round and needing a win to claim eighth position, attempted to grab an initiative with a short kick to restart. Just more than a minute remained. Similarly St Helens required a win by 10 points or more to gain home advantage in the play-offs by virtue of claiming the Super League runners-up spot. Ade Gardner anticipated the ploy and won the ball.

This final set of six were all Saints had. Four tackles on and 72 yards had been made. Cunningham waited to receive the ball from Tony Puletua and scurried towards the line. Though held up when he reached it, the hooker managed to wriggle free, touching down beneath the posts with 12 seconds on the clock. A simple conversion for Jamie Foster earned the necessary points advantage to pip Warrington Wolves.

Having gained that more preferable route towards the Grand Final and helped create three tries in the concluding competitive fixture at Knowsley Road – an eliminating semi-final play-off against Huddersfield Giants – Cunningham fittingly was the last player to cross the line. Once more it was a charge from short distance after taking the ball which saw the club captain squeeze in. Dilapidated as it may appear to some eyes, the old stadium still proved it had more magic and history inside it. It was a fitting end to its own time and the career of one of the club's most distinguished servants.

THE FINAL SCORE

St Helens will leave Knowsley Road, their home of 120 years, ahead of the 2011 Super League season. Though a Boxing Day friendly against Wigan Warriors may yet see the famous old stadium out; when the final play-off game against Huddersfield Giants was completed Saints' home record across all competitions was as follows:

	P	W	D	L	Pts F	Pts A
League	1704	1271	67	366	35293	16519
Championship	31	27	0	4	717	220
Play-offs	18	15	0	3	453	249
Premiership	22	18	1	3	587	265
Challenge Cup	113	85	6	22	2625	881
JPS/Regal Trophy	36	29	2	5	1058	459
Lancashire Cup	90	64	4	22	2012	912
Floodlit Trophy	32	28	0	4	679	297
World Club Championship	4	1	0	3	94	144
Yorkshire Cup	3	1	0	2	38	44
Western Division	10	9	0	1	273	74
War Emergency League	90	49	3	38	1071	894
Total	**2153**	**1597**	**83**	**473**	**44900**	**20958**